Pelican Books
Home and School

As a parent of children at playgroup and secondary
school, a former teacher and a member of an
education committee, Tyrrell Burgess is well
qualified to write on the subjects covered in
Home and School. He is head of the School for
Independent Study at the North East London
Polytechnic. He became a teacher after graduating
from Oxford and then news editor of *The Times
Educational Supplement*. He was the first director
of the Advisory Centre for Education, became
assistant editor of *New Society* and then did
research on educational institutions at the London
School of Economics and the North East London
Polytechnic. He has written numerous articles for
newspapers and specialist journals and his books
include *A Guide to English Schools* (published in
Penguins), *Inside Comprehensive Schools* and
*Policy and Practice: The Colleges of Advanced
Technology* (with John Pratt, Allen Lane The
Penguin Press).

Home
and
School

Tyrrell Burgess

Illustrated by Janet Turner

Penguin Books

Penguin Books Ltd,
Harmondsworth, Middlesex, England
Penguin Books Inc.,
7110 Ambassador Road, Baltimore, Maryland 21207, U.S.A.
Penguin Books Australia Ltd,
Ringwood, Victoria, Australia
Penguin Books Canada Ltd,
41 Steelcase Road West, Markham, Ontario, Canada
Penguin Books (N.Z.) Ltd,
182-190 Wairau Road, Auckland 10, New Zealand

First published in Great Britain by
Allen Lane The Penguin Press 1973
Published with revisions in Pelican Books 1976
Copyright © Tyrrell Burgess, 1973, 1976

Made and Printed in Great Britain by
Richard Clay (The Chaucer Press) Ltd,
Bungay, Suffolk
Set in Linotype Juliana

Contents

Introduction

Each child is unique. This is obvious and yet always astonishing; and we do well to remember it whenever we start to speak of children, schools or education. The individual child is, after all, what the whole process is about. And if we start from an individual child, most of us can quickly say what we most want for him: that he should grow and develop, physically, emotionally and mentally, so that he becomes an independent adult, the master and not the slave of circumstances. Education is what helps him to do this.

There is almost nowhere in the world where this job of education is done only by the isolated family of mother, father and brothers and sisters. An Indian child may be born into an extended family of parents, grandparents, uncles, aunts, cousins – all part of the surrounding village, caste or tribe. And in almost no society is education given over entirely to the state, so that parents see little of their children after they are born. Everywhere the job of education is shared by parents and society; shared in different ways, of course, from one place to another. In modern societies, like Britain, the upbringing of children is shared by parents and the state. The parents provide a home, and early upbringing; the state provides schools as children grow older. It even passes laws to make parents see that their children are educated. It is only recently that these two influences, the home and the school, have begun consciously to come together. In the past most parents scarcely thought of themselves as educating their children. That was a job, most of them thought, for the schools. And many schools shared this view, often regarding parents with open hostility. As we shall see, all this is changing, if perhaps too slowly for comfort.

This book has been written, first of all for parents: to explain to them what is going on in schools today. Often this is quite different from what they remember of their own schooldays, and their contacts with their children's schools can leave them baffled and bewildered. They may be anxious to help and take an interest but find it hard to take the first step. So the book offers them practical advice on what they can do to support their children at school, to help them to make the most of it. The book is also for teachers: to help them to see the parents' point of view and to suggest what they can do to involve parents in their children's education. What I hope to do is to help to bridge the gap between home and school to show parents and teachers what the other is doing and to suggest how both can collaborate in the upbringing of the child.

This book grew out of a series of articles commissioned for *New Society*, and I am grateful to the then editor, Timothy Raison, for all his help and encouragement. Shortly after they appeared I delivered a course of lectures for the southeastern district of the Workers' Educational Association, at the evening education centre, Hawkwood Lane, Chislehurst, Kent, and I must say here how grateful I am to the members of that course for showing me what really interested parents, rather than what mainly interested me. A friend of mine, reading the original articles, said doubtfully, 'You know, you *sound* a very good parent'. When I looked hurt, she added, 'Well, knowing the way you treat your own children . . .' . I can only thank them, and my wife, Joan, for putting up with it.

I am grateful for Eve Sears's valuable help in typing and checking proofs.

I must finally apologize to parents who have daughters, and who may get fed up with constant references to 'he' and 'him'. It is done for simplicity, and not out of prejudice.

1 How Children Grow and Develop

Before we can understand education, we must understand children. We need to know how children grow and develop, and we need to know this especially these days when so much of what happens in schools is based upon it. Most parents know, from experience of their own children, a very great deal about child growth. In some ways, this chapter will simply remind you of what you know already. But it will also show how this forms the basis of principles of growth, which in turn form the basis of educational theory and practice. There is a lot, of course, that we do not know about the growth and development of children. For example, we do not know whether repeated physical exercise in childhood hastens the growth of muscles or permanently affects their size. We know almost nothing about the growth of the brain after the age of two. But fortunately some facts are clear.

First, children grow more quickly at some stages than at others. They are growing most quickly at birth – at the rate of about eight inches a year (if they went on growing at that rate, they would be eight feet tall by the age of twelve!). By the age of three they are growing at two and a half inches a year, and for the next six years or so they grow even more slowly than that. After that, at adolescence, there is a very marked speeding up of growth (known as the 'adolescent spurt') when the child is again growing as fast as he was at the age of two.

Second, girls and boys differ markedly in the rates at which they develop. The average girl experiences her adolescent spurt between ten and a half and about thirteen: the average

boy between twelve and a half and fifteen. This means that
girls are for a time (say from eleven to fourteen) taller,
heavier, probably stronger and obviously sexually more developed. The boys 'catch up' and surpass the girls in both
body measurements and muscular strength about two years
later. But all this is true of 'average' children. Children of
the same age and sex differ enormously in their physical and
intellectual development. Parents realize this when they say
of a child, 'He's very tall for his age', or 'She's very bright
for a four-year-old', and teachers when they talk about 'late
developers'. The variations are most dramatic at adolescence.
One girl may have her first menstrual period at the age of
ten, another at sixteen and a half, and both are entirely normal girls. Similarly, of two fourteen-year-old boys, one may
be small and childlike, with a piping voice, undeveloped
reproductive organs and no body hair; the other may be a
beefy pillar of the football team, with a deep bass voice, a
stubborn beard and adult genitalia. These variations are in
physical development, but there are similar variations in
mental and emotional development too, and at all stages of
growth, not only at adolescence.

A third fact about children's growth is that it is taking
place more quickly. Children are maturing earlier: they are
getting older younger. In 1900 most English boys probably
stopped growing only at twenty-two; nowadays they are
usually fully grown by seventeen or eighteen. London five-
year-olds in 1959 were on average three inches taller than
those of 1910, and most of the difference was due to earlier
development. The age of the menarche (the first menstrual
period) has been falling by about four months every ten
years – recorded since the late 1940s in Britain, and ever
since 1850 in Norway. Nobody knows why this has happened,
but it is probably due to better food and home conditions,
particularly in early childhood. (Perhaps child development
was set back by the industrial revolution: Shakespeare's Juliet,
in *Romeo and Juliet*, was only 14.)

These facts have led biologists and psychologists to talk of a number of principles of growth. First, there is the idea of a 'developmental age' – meaning not the age a child is in years (which would be the chronological age) but the stage he has reached between birth and his full maturity: the point to which he has developed. This idea recognizes that for educational purposes it is not much use knowing that the two fourteen-year-old boys mentioned earlier are fourteen. This becomes an almost meaningless description: they are quite clearly at different stages of development, their 'developmental ages' are quite different and they should probably get quite different educational treatment. Should they, for example, do physical education together? In a child's physical development, this developmental age can be fairly easily estimated (it is commonly done by studying the bones of the wrist) and can be seen to follow a definite sequence of changes. A similar sequence is seen in tests of muscular control, and it is very likely that the principle applies in mental and emotional development too. The age at which a particular sequence begins, and the speed at which it proceeds, may vary from one child to another, but the sequence itself is the same: the changes take place in the same order.

The sequence in which the brain develops differs markedly from that of the rest of the body. Even before birth, the brain is nearer to its adult size than is any other organ except the eye. At the age of five, when a child is only two-fifths of his adult height, his brain is already nine-tenths of its adult weight. The functions of the brain depend upon its physical development. For example, some functions are localized in particular parts of the brain: one part is concerned with vision, another with movement and so on, and around these 'primary' areas there are other areas concerned with integrating the information arriving at the primary areas. The primary areas mature in a regular sequence. The first is the area concerned with movement, followed by those concerned with feeling, sight and hearing. We can say that waves of development spread out from the primary areas into the surrounding areas.

Even within the areas concerned with movement and feeling there is a localization of function to a part of the body. Brain cells near the top of the area, for example, serve the leg, those in the middle the hand and those at the bottom the tongue and mouth. These cells develop in the same sequence as the parts of the body to which they correspond. The arm cells, for example, develop ahead of the leg cells, just as a baby's arms are more advanced in growth than his legs. It is only after the physical developments have taken place in the brain that the brain functions appear. We know that this is the case up to the age of two; that, for example, a baby cannot focus his eyes on a distant object or blink at a moving object until the area of the brain concerned with sight has become sufficiently developed. And it is assumed that this kind of process continues, and that throughout development brain functions depend upon the brain's physical development. It is thought, for example, that the ability to think logically (at adolescence) comes only after other changes in the brain. Before the brain's physical developments have taken place, the mental functions cannot occur. A similar connection is visible in muscular control. A baby cannot be 'pot-trained' until his muscles are ready for him to control himself, and there is no point in trying.

The idea of a sequence of development has given rise to the principles of 'critical' or 'sensitive' periods: stages in development at which some outside influence may be crucial. Perhaps the most familiar example is the way in which German measles in the early months of pregnancy can cause defects in the unborn child. Another example is that nowadays psychologists feel fairly sure that a baby or young child 'expects' to be cuddled: if he is not cuddled at the appropriate stage, he may become seriously disturbed. This principle is a familiar one to teachers, who may feel that there is for every child a particular time when he might most easily learn, say, to read. It is not a question of 'now or never' – people are taught to read at all ages – but of being most ready at one stage and less ready at others. It has to be admitted that there is still too little evidence for anyone to be quite sure about this.

Perhaps the most relevant principle for this book is the new understanding of the influence of heredity and environment. This used to be known as the 'nature-nurture' controversy: were a child's characteristics due mostly to heredity or to upbringing? In a sense this was an argument about the value of education. If most of a child's characteristics were inherited, there was not much that education could do; if they were due to upbringing, then the more education the better. The argument, of course, was whether it was *mostly* one or the other. Nowadays the argument has been made redundant. Our characteristics are due, not to heredity, not to environment, nor even to a mixture of the two, but through the interaction of one with the other. Our genes (what we get from our fathers and mothers) are the essential basis for development, but they do not determine our characteristics. We do not inherit tallness or intelligence, just like that. What we inherit is a disposition to be tall (or whatever it is) in particular circumstances. In Britain, people with such a disposition would be likely actually to be tall, because most of them have enough to eat as children. But in countries where starvation and disease are common, they might not be so tall: they might be stunted, genes or no genes. On the other hand, not everyone is affected equally by adversity. In particular, girls stand malnutrition and illness better than boys do. So a child's characteristics are not innate, and a particular environment may be bad for a child with certain genes and good for a child with others. Deprivation might not mean the same for one child as another.

There is one area in which heredity and environmental influences are inextricably mixed up, and that is in the factor of social class. The differences between the classes are quite startling. The children of the well-off are larger than those of the poor. At the age of five, children from upper-middle-class homes are an inch taller on average than those from unskilled workers' homes, and one and a quarter or one and a half inches taller at adolescence.Children with many brothers and sisters tend to be smaller than those with few. Five-year-old London boys who are only children are on average one and a quarter inches taller than those with four or more brothers and sisters. Children from small families reach puberty earlier than those from large families. But it is not so much family income or father's occupation that operates here as attitudes and traditions of child care. It is amusing to notice that at any rate one study showed that gains in the height and weight of children in private boarding schools were only half as much in term time as in the holidays: due to malnutrition or psychological disturbance?

These, then, are the facts and principles of physical growth. They apply, too, to the growth of behaviour: each part of a child's behaviour results from the interaction of heredity, his own history and his immediate situation. Very few of a child's responses are innate (as are many of those of young birds): most require learning, though the basis on which learning takes place is inborn. For example, a baby from two to eight months old will smile at anything which looks like a pair of eyes on a face – a round card with two spots on it will do. Later he learns to distinguish his mother from other adults and smiles at her. Even later, the child or adult has a whole range of expressions to show friendliness, sympathy and so on. The point is that the baby needs stimulation from outside (in this case an actual mother or mother-substitute) if he is to develop properly. The stimulation has to be very varied and complex for the full range of normal behaviour.

The child himself has a very strong drive, from a very early age, towards activity and exploration. He is curious about new experiences. He shows a great drive to master the world around him, and does this largely by practice. To take a simple example, a small child tries to place one of his toy blocks on a table. At first he may push it too gently, so that it drops down on the floor. Or he may hurl it right across the other side. Gradually he learns the exact amount of effort needed to put it on the table and no more, and he does this over and over again. When he can really do it he loses interest. Children differ enormously, both in the rate at which their behaviour develops and also in the whole character of their response. Different children, even in the same family, often have different temperaments from birth, as any parent with more than one child knows. A parent's attitudes and personality interact with the child's temperament, with delightful or disastrous results as the case may be. Too little is known about the way in which these interactions affect different children. What is known is that learning is bound up with emotional stability. A child who does not achieve emotional control and satisfactory relationships with adults may refuse, or be unable, to learn.

Emotional development also takes place in a sequence. The very young baby has a general total response of comfort or discomfort involving the whole body and nervous system. He screams and coos, as it were, all over. By the end of his second year he can be seen to have specific emotions: anger, love, fear, jealousy, and so on. Even a five-year-old is still vulnerable to his emotions and remains subject to overpowering fears and impulses. Fears themselves change in sequence. A one-year-old fears unknown and sudden changes; later he fears specific things, like dogs or noisy engines; later still he fears things from his imagination and fantasies; at a later stage, though while still at primary school, his fears may be connected with personal experience, a sense of inadequacy or the need to be accepted.

Much early learning is concerned with helping the child to cope with his needs, impulses and fears, to live with others, accept delays and frustrations and build up inner controls. The child is not just 'trained': he learns to handle his feelings and drives himself. Take aggression, for example. A two-year-old has tantrums and fights for possession, a nursery school child has brief quarrels, an older junior school child engages in verbal insults. Aggression is necessary, to enable the individual to assert his identity in society, and children learn to expose their aggression in socially acceptable ways. In all this, the dependence of the child on the adults around him is of critical importance. We now know the consequences of a child's being deprived of love and affection at an early age. Such a child may find difficulty in handling his own impulses and drives, may very well find all learning hard or impossible. Equally, the overprotected child may also have difficulty in learning.

There is a sequence too in the social development of children. At fifteen to eighteen months, a child recognizes and responds to other children. Between two and three and a half he plays as an individual, alongside rather than with other children. It is odd to watch a couple of three-year-olds in the same room, each going about his own business, talking to himself rather than to his companion. Even at four or five a group of children will disintegrate if left without an adult. It is between the ages of eight and twelve that a child learns to live and play in cooperation and competition in what are known as 'peer' groups of children of his own age. Here is where he learns to control his feelings and establish roles and social techniques and become accepted for what he is and what he can do.

Moral development is closely linked with emotional and social development: a young child acts within rules laid down by others even if he often breaks them. He is governed by the approval and disapproval of those around him. People tell him what is right and wrong. Later, in a peer group, children make their own rules which may be modified by common agreement. A lot of children from eight onwards love making up games with elaborate rules. But even the eleven-year-old has only a pretty crude sense of justice. It is only at adolescence that anything like an independent 'conscience' is developed.

We have seen how children grow and develop. What does it all imply for parents? Perhaps understanding can relieve parents of some of their more common worries. People with more than one child know how much children differ. They are often amazed that they managed to produce such opposites. They see, too, that their second child walked or talked months earlier or later than their first. It is comforting to know that this is entirely normal, and that if a child seems less developed than his contemporaries this is no immediate cause for alarm. It cannot matter (except to the comfort of mothers) whether a child is pot-trained early or late, and there is no harm (except to the self-esteem of some fathers) if a boy is not one of the brawnier footballers in the school.

Nor need parents be too astonished if they get on with one child better than another. Arrant favouritism is not a good thing (as the innumerable children's stories make clear) but parents need not feel guilty if they actually like one child more than another. That is what you would expect. Indeed, too literal equality of treatment can be quite wrong. Children have different needs, and what may be good for one may be bad for another: try to be fair, rather than unvarying.

Children are people, and deserve to be treated as such. There are some, relatively rich, fathers who put their son's name down for their old school as soon as he is born. This is an affront, and the schools are wrong to encourage it. How can they tell what sort of school will be suitable for the boy in thirteen years' time? There are also parents who feel that, because an elder child went to a certain school, the younger children should too. This feeling is particularly acute when the younger fails to get into a grammar school, but it happens at other times too, and is normally irrational. Try to think of the child as an individual, not just a chip off the old block. All this has been somewhat negative: but, of course, knowledge about the way children grow and develop can help parents to make a home environment which provides the right stimulus when a child is ready for it. Some indication of what they can do will be found in the later chapters of this book.

But what we know about children's growth has implications for teachers and school as well. If we take the idea of the developmental age seriously, then the way schools are at present organized can be seen to present difficulties. Children in most schools are grouped together according to their chronological ages. They 'go up' from one class to another year by year, and they all transfer from primary to secondary school at the same age. Yet this must do some injustice to some children. Again, many secondary schools are coeducational even though at puberty girls are on average two years ahead of boys developmentally. This is not just a matter of educational theory. A parent may feel that the school, or the whole educational system, is too rigid at times and that his own child is suffering from this because he is ahead or behind in development. At this point the facts and principles of growth and their consequences become visible in the individual child, and teachers, schools and systems alike should be flexible enough to allow for this. In a later chapter we shall see what a parent can do if they are not.

Above all, though, what parents can provide, as nobody else can, is the physical and emotional security which are so necessary for growth. Fortunately, rank malnutrition (which retards development) is comparatively rare in Britain; but as we have seen, physical differences in children are related to home circumstances. Much has been said about social class and the size of families in this connection, but I ought to emphasize that it is home conditions, rather than economic circumstances, which are important. It is not wealth, but habits of regular meals, sleep and general organization which distinguish the 'good' family. Similarly, physical growth and behavioural and emotional development can be hindered by psychological disturbance. We know the importance of the loving care which the normal child can count on from studies of those children who have been deprived of it. Again, it is the emotional climate of the home that is important, not specific techniques of child-rearing. As for the latter, there can be almost no method that will not work with some parents.

This conclusion may disappoint you: it seems a long way to have to come to discover that the best thing is to do what comes naturally: to look after children, feed them, clothe them, love them. These are things which parents do naturally, normally without thought of education or school, for their child's sake. Just as the child was conceived in an act of love of his parents, so their mutual love is needed for his successful development. But we live in a complex society, so it is a help if love is accompanied by understanding of the way children grow, of their needs for development and of their progress to independence. If parents have this they will find that, willy-nilly, they have laid a good foundation for the school then to share the task of helping their children to maturity.

2 The Pre-School Years

There has probably never been a time when parents have been better, on the whole, than they are today. They can seldom have been more conscientious, and they have certainly never had so much good advice. Whole generations have been brought up on Dr Spock, whose book, *Baby and Child Care*, begins with that perfect sentence, 'You know more than you think you do.' It is not my job to repeat all the good advice about diet, pot-training, dummies, afternoon sleeps and so on which goes into the rearing of so many babies. The homes of most children are good and loving, which is what matters most, even though it is not all that matters.

But there are one or two things to be said about a child's early years, before he goes to school, and about the purpose and possibilities of nursery schools. The first of these is about play. A lot of parents miss the point of this: they say that children are 'just playing' and imply that it is all frivolity. Such parents are often shocked when they see what goes on in infant schools these days: 'It's all play,' they say. But play is work. Through it a child learns. He learns to use his body, and he practises physical skills. He learns to understand himself and the world around him. Sometimes he acts out scenes which please or frighten him, sometimes he tries on adult roles for size. He is expanding his mental capacities, his imagination. He is growing emotionally and socially. Every day he tries to do something more difficult or something that older children or adults do. It may be that it is only recently that the importance of play has been consciously recognized – though we need not go as far as a recent Sunday paper which gave as an example of 'new' educational methods the stringing of a row of beads across a baby's cot, a device which goes back to the Stone Age. This ought to warn us not to get too pompous about play. But many parents find it hard to let children simply get on with it. They may buy a new doll's house, but then get in the way by pointing out that this is the bedroom, and the basin goes in the bathroom – no not *there*, that's the garage. Too many fathers, frustrated in their own childhood, buy expensive train sets too early, and then bully their sons mercilessly if they so much as tread on the level crossing. All this makes play no fun and makes children feel incompetent. The thing to do (as I have now learnt) is to let the children show you what they are doing and how to do it.

Another important factor in the years before school is the child's growing grasp of language. This is coming to be seen as extremely important both to intellectual development and to success at school. Some parents, whose own education was pretty ragged, may use a very limited range of words: highly educated parents may use a very wide vocabulary. The difference is not just a matter of precocious brats coming out with long words (like the infant Macaulay who was faced with some kind but patronizing inquiry, like, 'Is iddums diddums toofipegs better den?' and replied, 'Indeed, Madam, the agony is somewhat abated'). The importance of words is that we use them to think with, and a child with a very restricted vocabulary is chained to a very narrow and concrete view of life. At the same time, a child needs to have built up a vocabulary if he is to learn to read. This happens quite quickly in normal children, who know about 2,000 words by the age of about five. It has been suggested that a child needs about 3,000 words to begin reading. It may sound trite to assert that one of the best ways of preparing a child for school is to talk to him and to read to him, but it is nonetheless true. It is, I confess, sometimes a bore. Children do not infallibly enjoy what interests their parents. My own children have been read to indefatigably by their grandparents – a solution which is virtually ideal for all concerned.

A third pre-school need is what used to be called discipline, but I mean this to include the way a child behaves to his parents, to other children and to familiar and unfamiliar adults. A lot of teachers complain these days that children will not listen when spoken to and thus need to be nagged, and I do not think this is just a hangover from the days of Queen Victoria. My own theory is that many parents have been slightly brainwashed into permissiveness. I am sure one ought to be friendly to children, but I am equally sure that parents have rights. There ought not to be nightly arguments about going to bed, cleaning teeth or whatever. There is no need for children to have a general licence to destroy the furniture and draw on the walls – though there should be somewhere, if possible, where they can do both. Children should not jump on visitors. Six-year-olds should be ready to tidy up their things when they have finished with them, though I am all for not doing it too often, and I do not think children have the stamina for it at an earlier age. The ideal is to be both friendly and firm. If one can be, the child knows where he is and learns to get on with people. A spoilt child is not necessarily happy and may have formidable problems later on. Parents need to maintain their self-respect.

It helps in all this if father is present and actively helping with discipline. It is difficult if he comes in at the end of a long day wanting only the evening paper, but finds wife and children somewhat bedraggled. Boys and girls need their father both as a companion and as a parent, not just as a remote figure. If both parents can enjoy their children, find them pleasant to have around, and avoid guilt about their own inevitable periods of anger, they may well find that other people, including teachers, will find their children pleasant too. This is not a book about upbringing, but it would be wrong not to mention hitting children. Some people think this is the ultimate in cowardly bullying, others do it all the time. I can only say that I have frequently struck my own children in anger, on occasions with a slipper. (My wife on one well-remembered occasion used a hairbrush.) But I find that I hit children much less often as they get older. Cynics would no doubt say that I beat them when they are helpless and stop when they get in sight of hitting back – but I think it is rather that as they get older they become more amenable to reason. One doesn't find the same need to thump. But, of course, punishment is never the main element in discipline: what keeps the child on the rails most of the time is a stable and loving family.

Space for play, a literate background, a friendly but firm regime: some homes manage themselves all this and more. Most of us seek help outside. Our young children need somewhere to play that is safe and in which they can make a mess, they need the company of other children and of adults other than their parents with whom they can strike up less emotionally charged relationships. It may be that all these needs can be met in an idyllic South Sea island: palm-fringed beaches make a natural playground where children can run, jump and climb, make, destroy and pretend at will; other children, of all ages, are legion; the extended family provides innumerable adults of receding degrees of kinship. But Britain is not like this: it is a damp area too far north whose people have accumulated in vast and overcrowded expanses of industrial and other man-made squalor. In these circumstances, all our children are deprived. Think for a moment of the child in a desirable suburban semi-detached house. He is scarcely in opulence. He may have a bedroom in which his toys are kept, but (especially if there is more than one bed) there will be very little room for play. Downstairs he will be lucky to have the intermittent use of the narrow hall and perhaps one room. None of these spaces has been designed for him and are likely to be full of things which he is forbidden to touch and which may kill or maim him if he does. He may have a strip of garden – but how much of that may he play on and dig up? A child in a much bigger house and garden may gain in space and lose through isolation. On the other hand, a child in a slum may have plenty of chums and an extended family at hand and a safe enough street to play in but his home may be overcrowded and poor. The child in a flat, whether luxury or council, may get the worst of both worlds: constriction and isolation together. But all these children have typical British homes. All need more as a home than post-industrial Britain can provide. The pioneers of nursery education set out to remedy a social evil: the appalling lives of children in slums; but nursery schools are still needed by most children. It is worth remembering, here, that children are maturing earlier. A child of four and a half today is as mature as a five-year-old between the wars. If five was the right age to start school then, the right age today would be six months earlier. There are a very great many pre-school children who are 'ready' for school.

I have been talking as if every normal child is in some sense deprived. But, of course, children from shared houses and broken homes or with inadequate parents or obsessive mothers are even more obviously so. If the growth of measured intelligence is associated with social and economic background, poor children need enrichment. If poverty of language is a cause of poor achievement children with inarticulate parents need educated and trained help as soon as appropriate. And it is not only children who are deprived. In an isolated family a mother often has no respite from her children, no chance for contacts outside her home. Many mothers feel guilty about resenting this, as if women throughout the ages have managed, and why shouldn't they? The answer to this is that, of course, a lot of mothers simply did not manage, but nobody noticed; and traditional societies have always supported the individual mother with all manner of grandmothers, aunts and so on. In a fairly primitive village the children are not 'under foot' all day as they are in a modern house or flat. A mother can be better if she is less weary and more help to her children if she has taken up outside interests. Nor need she feel guilty about going out to work – provided the children are satisfactorily settled down with relatives, friends or a nursery school. There have been some studies done on children whose mothers are working, and these found that there was no noticeable difference in general stability and happiness between those children whose mothers were at home all the time and those whose mothers were consistently out at work. The children who suffered were those whose mothers went out intermittently to work: they were affected in the same ways as children with unpredictable parents and home circumstances. Some mothers have to work: they may be alone and thus the only earner. But many go to work because they want to, either because they enjoy it or because they want the extra income. Such mothers, in particular, may seek the nursery school for their children.

I ought to say, though, that there are still people who argue against nursery education. What they say is that the place of the young child is with his mother at home. They add that some children are harmed by too early a removal from their mother's care and companionship and that the anxiety which this sets up works against healthy independence, making the child either too clinging or too detached and unable to form relationships with others. It is true that some children are ready earlier than others to spend part of the day away from home. But this is an argument for being sure to treat each child as an individual, not deciding that no child shall go to a nursery school. In this, as in so many things, you have to trust parents and teachers.

This raises the question of the age at which a child should go to nursery school. From what I have just said, it will be clear that some will say as late as possible. But there can be no rule about it. Many, perhaps most, children are 'ready' at three, others not until later. Some parents will boast that their daughter went at two or three and a half. If she enjoyed it, so well and good.

A good nursery school sees itself as 'a complement to the home, never a substitute', as one experienced teacher put it. Something of this may be seen in the way a nursery school admits a child. While he is on the waiting list (which, as we shall see, can sometimes be very long) his mother may be asked to call in with him once or twice when she is passing. He is thus familiar with the school by the time he is formally admitted. His mother is likely to be invited to stay on the first day and perhaps for an hour or two on subsequent days. Some children are happy to be left completely after a day or two, others take a week or more. Often it is the child who administers the tactless but encouraging dismissal, 'Why don't you go home now mummy, like all the other mummys?' Much depends on your own attitude. Some mothers get very fraught at the moment of leaving their infant for the first time, so it is not surprising if the child balks at it. If you are reluctant to leave him, he will imagine that there's nothing worse than to be left. When the time comes to go, go. Don't mess about but go as if you meant to come back, not as if this were good-bye for ever.

What does a good nursery school offer? First a physical environment: there is space to play, indoors and out. There will be plenty to do: a good deal of water, clay, sand and paint, and pieces of large equipment, like climbing frames and boxes. There will be books, perhaps pets, clothes for dressing up in. You are likely to find the children pottering, or rushing about, largely on their own. Some of them will have very short spans of concentration, and move from one thing to another quite quickly. An individual child may spend the whole morning on one painting. They are not all likely to be doing the same thing. But the children are not just on their own. The second thing a good nursery school offers is the skilled help of trained teachers. The more unobtrusive this is the better, but if you watch the teacher carefully during a visit you will see that she is not only available when wanted by the children for advice or help, she is also keeping a very swift moving eye on what is happening, ready to intervene, to encourage or simply to talk. A good teacher spends part of every day with each individual child, in however offhand a way she may seem to do it. At intervals, the children may sit together on the floor for singing or to hear a story.

Parents often worry that children are not learning anything at nursery school: a friend's four-year-old may be beginning to write while their own does not. A level-headed acceptance of the fact that children differ comes in handy here. But in any case, formal learning (of multiplication tables and the alphabet, for instance) is not what nursery schools are for. A four-year-old may get to recognize simple words, form letters, know that two and three make five, but he may not. He is very busy learning other things and can be left to get on with them. As I said earlier, play is a serious business. One indication that the children are indeed hard at work lies in the fact that many are quite tired by lunch-time. Nursery schools often have bunks in which the children can lie down, especially during the afternoon. Many parents and teachers prefer children to attend part-time only. Again, there can be no rule (working mothers may have to leave children full-time) except to watch the child. If he is seriously weary, perhaps he should go less often. Some children seem tired after the first few days but soon adjust later. Consult the teacher if you are in doubt.

Teachers at nursery schools are often almost lyrical about what they are doing. They speak (I have heard them) of liberating a child's spirit, of never under-rating his intelligence, of encouraging his search for truth. The children are at school to create and explore, to answer or partly answer their own questions – and in this way they develop physically, mentally, spiritually, emotionally, aesthetically. A nursery school, they say, 'is a way of life'. Well, that may seem rather high-falutin' for what your child does for three hours every morning. But nursery schools and their teachers and pioneers have had such a large and beneficial influence on

British education that they deserve a little exaltation. In any case, the thing to do is see for yourself.

But there is the trouble. It is something of a let-down after all this to discover how few nursery schools there are. In England and Wales there are some 530 'maintained' nursery schools (those run by local authorities) with 15,000 full time and 24,000 part time pupils and nursery classes with 73,000 children. There are just over 100 private nursery schools with 2,500 full time and 2,200 part time pupils. This means that there is a place in a nursery school or class for fewer than seven children in every hundred. There are also a number of day nurseries in most towns. People often ask what the difference is between a day nursery and a nursery school. The difference lies in the word 'school'. A day nursery meets a social need: it minds children while their parents are at work. A nursery school meets an educational need: it is concerned with the growth and development of children. A nursery school operates for the normal school hours (or less) and terms: a day nursery is usually open longer than normal working hours (for obvious reasons) and is open all the year round. You pay according to your income for a place in a local authority day nursery: its nursery schools are free. The day nursery is the responsibility of the health, not the education, authorities. There may be 75,000 children in these day nurseries.

You can find out about maintained nursery schools from the local education office (address from the local telephone book, or local library) which ought also to have some information about private nursery schools. The health visitor is often knowledgeable too. Otherwise you may have to rely for information on other parents and the local gossip. There are no fees for maintained nursery schools: in the private ones the fees may be anything from a lowish 25p a morning or £1 a week (say £15 a term) to a rarer 50 or 75 guineas a term or more. There was small hope for any significant expansion of nursery education, even though the Plowden Report (*Children and their Primary Schools*) recommended it. The shortage was for a long time governed by a circular from the Department of Education and Science which said that, because of the shortage of teachers for primary schools, the local authorities could not expand nursery education. Later local authorities were allowed to establish nursery schools if this would free married women for teaching in other schools, but few authorities did so. Since 1969 there has been a programme for establishing nursery schools and classes in deprived areas, but this still falls far short of the Plowden recommendations. The main expansion has been in part time places.

In view of all this, most parents have to consider alternatives. Some mothers have turned to self-help. A remarkable movement, known as the Pre-School Playground Association, was started eleven years ago by a charmingly determined mother, Belle Tutaev. It now has about 8,500 playgroups associated with it and brings out a monthly magazine called *Contact* to keep them in touch with one another, as well as many other publications. A playgroup is not a nursery school, though some aspire to be as much like one as possible, with fully trained teachers. Many of them are run by mothers, sometimes taking turns. Many try to involve mothers in the running of the group even when there is a permanent leader. Some playgroups have been able to provide themselves with spacious and attractive accommodation and expensive equipment; others make do with someone's large front room or a church hall and build up their stock of equipment only gradually. Most of them are part time: they run for two or three hours in a morning, or for two or three mornings a week. They may charge from 5p an hour to 50p a morning. A playgroup is what the name implies: a place where children can play safely with more space and more challenge than they may get at home, alongside other children and with adults other than their parents. If you want to start, or help to start, a playgroup, perhaps the best thing to do is to write to and join the Pre-School Playgroups Association. You will find some of the Administrative requirements daunting otherwise. Briefly, you should apply to the local medical officer of health. A playgroup in someone's home must be registered as a 'childminder', one in a hall as a day nursery. Normally the medical officer will inspect the premises, looking particularly at the space available, lavatory and washing facilities, safety – of stairs, outside steps and heating – and will fix a limit to the number of children who may be accepted and say how many adults there should be with them. Town planning permission should be obtained from the local planning department. (One mother, faced with the objection that 'This is a residential area', exclaimed, 'Well, where else would you have a playgroup?') It would also be sensible to have the place inspected by the local fire station.

Although the playgroup movement grew because of the shortage of nursery schools, it has evolved its own distinctive approach. The most important aspect of this concerns the place of parents. Mothers help to organize and run playgroups, not just because there is nobody else, but because that is part of the point of a playgroup. It involves mothers in planning and organizing to meet their own needs, and it gives them the chance to see their children with others and to learn from this. Many local associations of playgroups have arranged short courses of training for mothers in their groups. In short, the playgroup movement is a branch of adult education as well as pre-school experience.

I myself believe that the potential for playgroups is even more important than is generally recognized. There has always been something odd in the argument that the home environment is of such importance that we must have more nursery schools. The latter are usually very friendly places, but they are still *schools*. Playgroups offer a way of helping the *home*, through involving mothers (and indeed fathers) in providing for the play needs of their own children. In this, parents can learn quite as much as their children.

Naturally a child's pre-school education does not simply cease if he does not go to a nursery school or playgroup. It continues at home. The child's needs remain the same, though it may be harder to meet them. When parents ask what they can do, they may be disappointed by the humdrum sound of the replies. Parents (all parents, including busy executive fathers) can talk more to their children. If you are taking a child shopping, explain what you are doing, where you are going, what you are going to buy and why. Try to answer his paralysingly boring questions, particularly the ones which are too difficult. In small houses or flats it is hard to find a corner where a child can make a mess with water or paints: try to let him where possible, in the bathroom or kitchen (I am conscious that many families have neither). It is equally hard to find a corner where he can keep a lot of junk – old boxes and cartons, blocks and bricks, pieces of paper and cloth, the odd toy and so on. Try to find a part of a cupboard, or a trunk under his bed, or something which is his private horde of old rubbish. Of course, if you can spend some time with him, letting him help to make a doll from an empty detergent carton, so much the better. For this purpose some of those afternoon television programmes for children are full of bright and useful ideas. Open space may be scarce in a city or suburb: all the more reason for taking the child to a park as often as possible. It is a good thing to make a regular habit of this if you can. And some mothers may have to make a special effort to end their household isolation, for their own sakes as well as their children's. It is a help if you can form a circle of friends who invite each other round for coffee or tea. It's the change, as they say, that makes the difference.

3 Choosing a School

Before plunging into the business of starting at school, I want to pause and consider what sort of choice of school parents have. Many parents feel intimidated by the education service, and many authorities and schools encourage this feeling by keeping parents at a distance. This is what you might expect when an individual human need is met by an institution or by state provision. But you might like to be reminded that under the Education Act, 1944 (the foundation of the modern education service) the duty of seeing that your child is educated is laid squarely upon you! To be precise, the Section 36 of the Act says: 'It shall be the duty of the parent of every child of compulsory school age to cause him to receive efficient full time education suitable to his age, ability and aptitude, either by regular attendance at school or otherwise.' In practice this means that you must not only see that the child gets the education, but if he is at school you have to see he attends regularly.

The local education authorities have quite different duties. They must provide enough suitable schools and colleges in their area, so that a parent can fulfil *his* duty and then ensure that he does so. The natural duty of the parent towards his child is reinforced by law. The schools and the whole administrative apparatus behind them are a *service*.

Parents who pay fees for their children's education naturally treat the schools as a service: they assume they are free to choose one school rather than another. They assume that, if something is going wrong with their children's education, it is just as likely to be the school's fault, and may take the child away and put him somewhere else. This attitude, that the schools exist for the benefit of children and their parents, is the right one, and parents who use the state schools should share it. Most people are a bit confused about their rights to choose. Some parents believe that head teachers have the power to admit or reject; others that the 1944 Act gives them a specific right of choice. Both these beliefs are wrong, even though the official Plowden Committee made this mistake over choice. If they can be wrong, you might think, what chance have parents?

Let us see what Section 76 of the Act actually says: 'In the exercise and performance of all powers and duties conferred and imposed on them by this Act the Minister and local education authorities shall have regard to the general principle that, so far as is compatible with the provision of efficient instruction and the avoidance of unreasonable public expenditure, pupils are to be educated in accordance with the wishes of their parents.'

Now let us see what it does *not* say. It does not say that pupils *must* be educated according to their parents' wishes (even subject to the hefty qualifications about efficiency and expense). It does not even say that the authorities must *follow* the principle that they should be so educated. It merely says that they must have regard to this principle, and of course they can have regard to other things as well and can make exceptions to the general principle. And the qualifications are important: compatibility with efficient instruction implies that you can't make the authority put your child in an overcrowded school, even though you want it: and avoiding unreasonable expense would prevent your making the authority pay fees at the school of your choice if it were independent. And remember that the authorities can act only if they have the power or duty to do so. You cannot make them do something which is outside their powers. Finally, it is likely that Section 76 is not about choosing a school at all (it certainly does not mention this), but about children not being forced into things which their parents object to once they are *in* a school. The Section was slipped into the Act in the House of Lords as an extra protection from religious intolerance. So it is not surprising that parents who have taken local authorities to court have found Section 76 a broken reed. Similarly, appealing to the Minister under Section 68 of the Act, which says that the Minister may intervene if the local authority is acting 'unreasonably', normally gets you nowhere. The Minister will not normally interfere in something which is within the local authority's discretion. And an appeal under another section, Section 99, on the grounds that the authority is failing in its duty, has to rely on arguing that it is failing in its duty under Section 76 – and we are back where we started.

At this point you may feel that there is nothing much in the way of choice in the state system of education. But I have so far been talking only about the rights you can insist on in law. In practice, there can be a good deal of choice, and there could be more if parents showed clearly that they wanted it. At one time the Department of Education and Science published a *Manual of Guidance Schools* No. 1, dealing with the administration of Section 76, which gives some help. This said, reasonably enough, that authorities can and do safely assume that most parents will send their children to their local school, but added, 'There is, of course, no reason why parents should not send their children to another school of their choice if they wish to do so and if their choice is compatible with the conditions in Section 76.' It then set out for the local authorities 'some of the relevant considerations which may need to be balanced against each other before a decision is reached' on a parent's choice of school. Among these, the reasons for choosing an alternative school which the Department then listed have come to be recognized as reasonable grounds for doing so. Denominational considerations are among the strongest, and this has been recognized by the authorities. They regard it as obviously reasonable for parents to choose a Roman Catholic or Church of England school. What people do not realize, often, is that you do not have to belong to the denomination of the school you choose, though I suppose the authorities would regard this as evidence of the seriousness of your request. Still, religious or not, you can reasonably ask for a church school. A second 'no less strong' reason is the provision of a particular type of advanced work in a particular school. In practice this relates almost solely to sixth-form work, where there is rarely any difficulty anyway. Convenience of access to the school and the avoidance of traffic dangers is another possible reason, and here the Department agreed that there might be a case for letting a younger child go to the same school as an older brother or sister who can act as escort (providing they are both of an appropriate age). Parents may reasonably choose between a single-sex and a mixed school, may want a particular school because of their family's association with it or for medical reasons. (It would obviously be better for a crippled child to go to a school on one floor.) If one school offers school lunches and mother is out at work, it is reasonable to let the child go there; and in Wales, where linguistic passions may run high, you can choose for your child to be instructed in English or Welsh.

Given all these reasonable grounds for choosing one school rather than another, why should a local authority refuse a parent's wishes? Well, most of them try to be helpful, even if few positively try to encourage parental choice. There are two main reasons why an authority might refuse. The first is connected with the eleven plus procedures and selection for different kinds of secondary schools. There will be more about this in Chapter 7. For the moment it is enough to say that, if your child has not been selected for a grammar school (has not 'passed his eleven plus' as people say), you cannot choose a grammar school for him. This would be incompatible with the provision of efficient instruction, and it would not be 'suitable', to his ability and aptitude. The notion that certain schools are suitable only for particular children is becoming rapidly discredited, but while selection at eleven lasts you cannot get your child into a grammar school unless he scores highly enough on the tests, though you can try to prove that the test result did not do him justice.

The other reason why an authority may refuse a parent's choice of school is that the school in question is overcrowded. 'Overcrowded' is, of course a very flexible term, especially since many classes have more children in them than they should have. (The regulations used to say that there should be no more than forty children in a primary school class and thirty in a secondary: the new regulations were more vague, but the intention was the same.) But the *Manual of Guidance* said it was not compatible with the provision of efficient instruction if the school of the parent's choice is overcrowded, and recognized that authorities might have to 'zone' their schools to prevent this happening. Zoning is simply a matter of limiting the areas which are served by different schools, and turning away pupils from outside these areas. Zoning should take place only where it is unavoidable and should be ended as soon as possible, though this is not always done. Parents who come up against zoning arrangements may feel, either that it is a lot of old bureaucracy or that one extra child could not make all that much difference. Of course, some local authorities cope with sudden shifts in population better than others. But in general it is hard to argue with a zoning scheme – partly because there really is no use appealing to the Secretary of State about it.

The *Manual of Guidance* has recently been withdrawn but in practice its grounds of choice are still recognized by local authorities. If you want an alternative school to one you dislike, base your request upon them. Argue that you prefer the school of your choice for denominational, educational or co-educational reasons. These are the hardest to refuse. It is normally not much use saying that you reject a school because it is no good. In the first place, the officials are unlikely to agree, and some of them may deny that any of their schools is worse than another. In the second place, even if the school is appalling it is not clear why some other child should go there rather than yours. In other words, you might want to campaign for improvement, but in any appeal you would find it hard to argue that the authority was acting unreasonably in allocating your child a place. It is much easier to argue unreasonable behaviour if the authority is overriding an educational or denominational preference. It is a matter of tactics, of course, but you are likely to be on safer grounds if you stick to those which the Department considers reasonable.

Parents often feel instinctively that the person to get in touch with on a matter of this sort is the headmaster of the school of their choice. Talk to him, of course, and ask his advice, but you will find that in a case of dispute he will defer to the education office. He cannot normally take your part against them, not because he is craven but because this is their responsibility. The thing to do is write to the local chief education officer or director of education. You may find it convenient to set out very briefly your case in your letter: a couple of paragraphs is enough. Ask for a personal appointment with him or his deputy. One thing a headmaster will be able to tell you is the name of the key officer in question: ring him up and say that a letter is on its way through the chief officer.

In the interview itself, do not be shy of having your request mapped out on a sheet of paper. This is a serious business, and you cannot be expected to remember everything. Make a note of the replies too. You may get what you want. You may be offered a compromise: the school of your choice really is bursting at the seams, but there is yet another school, a little further away which is as good if not better . . . . Remember that the purpose of the exercise is to do the right thing for the child. Do not carry on the battle for its own sake. But you may, of course, meet a blank refusal. What can you do? If you are ready for it, you can always look for a fee-paying school. I know that most people feel that they cannot afford it, but there are some local day schools which charge surprisingly low fees: the equivalent of £1.50 a week. On the other hand, they may be no good either.

Can you fight the authority's decision? The answer is yes, but not hopefully. The first thing to do is to exhaust all the channels of local government. The last word locally comes not from the education office, but from the education committee, which is made up of councillors and coopted members. You can get onto any of them either direct or through your local councillor. One of the disadvantages of the lack of interest in local elections is that people do not naturally think of their councillors as people who can help them. But a councillor can and will take up your case in local government, much as an M.P. will with the national government. If you do not get anywhere with the committee or the council, you can write to the Secretary of State, through your M.P. if necessary; but as I have already explained this is not likely to get you very far. A note about councils and committees and how to find out who is on them will be found in Chapter 12.

Even when all this has failed, some parents still want to know if they can go further. They can, but it is not a comfortable process. What happens is this. I mentioned earlier that it is the parent's duty to see that his child is educated. Now, if the local authority offers your child a school you disapprove of and will not offer him the school of your choice, the first thing to do is to keep the child at home. (An alternative is to take him daily to the school you want and have him daily turned away: this is no more effective, and a good deal more humiliating to him, than keeping him at home.) What you are doing in effect is telling the authority that you are breaking the law. And the thing is that the authority has to do something about it. It cannot just let you stew in your own juice. It must first send you a notice requiring you to satisfy it that the child is receiving full-time education etc. You ignore this. The authority then sends a more formidable notice that it is going to serve on you (fourteen days later) a School Attendance Order. But it is at this point that you have the opportunity to assert your choice. This second notice gives you the right to select the school you wish your child to attend: to nominate the school named in the Order. Now the authority may disapprove of your choice (it probably will, since this is what the fight is about), but in order to deny your choice it has to appeal to the Minister. The onus of appeal, in other words, is now on the authority, not on you. And the authority can appeal only on relatively narrow grounds: that the school you have chosen is not suitable to your child or involves unreasonable public expenditure. The Secretary of State has the last word in this. If he rules for the authority, the school they choose will be the one named in the Order. If you defy the Order, you will be taken to court and you may find it hard to get the judge to let you bring all the circumstances of your dispute into the argument. If the courts acquit you, they could order that the School Attendance Order is no longer in force. And then we are back where we started. But it would be a pretty stiff-necked local authority that did not agree to your wishes at this stage. This procedure will only operate when a child starts at school or changes schools at eleven plus. You cannot take a child's name off the register of a school without the consent of the local authority: if you did so and kept the child at home, the authority would simply take you straight to court without the advantage of the attendance order procedure.

This process that I have outlined here is long and difficult. It is almost a war of attrition. The child suffers, from being singled out, from missing school and so on. The whole thing is inadvisable. Yet the local authority, or the parent, may go only part of the way before deciding that enough is enough. Authorities do not enjoy appeals to the Secretary of State, or being taken through the courts.

There is one final point. What about the parent who does not want a child to go to school at all? If you provide a tutor at home, that is of course all right, because the 1944 Act says you may see that the child is educated at school 'or otherwise'. But suppose you disagree with the formal education altogether. Only one parent, to my knowledge, has tried to keep her children at home like this. Mrs Joy Baker fought the Norfolk County Council for eight years, in the course of which she was fined and sentenced to imprisonment (which she avoided on appeal), and had to meet the Council's attempt to make her children wards of court. She argued that schools were a bad thing and that her children could be seen to be 'educated', even though they got no formal instruction. She herself was not a trained teacher and encouraged the children to follow their own interests. The moral of this is that you can refuse to send your children to school provided you are prepared to fight the authorities for at least eight years.

Let us suppose, then, that after all your efforts (however far you went), your child is going to some school other than the one of your choice. The thing to do is make the best of it. It really does no good to go on nagging about it. Your child will know that you don't like the school, which is undermining enough to his self-confidence. Indeed, the ill-effects of the whole battle may last much longer than the battle itself. What you have to do now is to help him to get the most out of the inevitable. Visit the school; treat it as if it is what you want. Try to understand what it is doing, and try to cooperate with it.

But let us now assume happier circumstances in which there is the possibility of choice. How do you go about choosing a school? However doubtful you may feel about it, nobody can do it for you. Choosing a school is a matter of matching two uniques, a child and a school. It can be done only by someone with an intimate knowledge of both. Parents know their own children better than anyone else can, at least from one point of view. You know whether he is boisterous and outgoing, ready to meet adults and other children, or quiet and timid, shrinking from new acquaintances; whether he concentrates on one thing for hours or turns quickly from one interest to another. You see his interests developing as he grows older. You may know less about what he is like away from home, but you can supplement your own knowledge with what other adults and teachers say about him, or by seeing how he performs in school competitions and examinations. If you are really in doubt, you may call in an expert like a child psychologist.

It is not at all easy to get to know schools. Many parents rely heavily on hearsay, which can be unreliable. The fact that all one's friends recommend a particular school is no guarantee that it will suit one's own child. Even the opinions of teachers can be misleading: it is often surprising how little teachers know of schools other than their own. A parent's opinion of a school may be based on little more than rumour, a quick general impression and the absence of obvious catastrophe – to his own child. Most parents quickly accept and defend their child's school, whatever their initial expectations and whatever the school does. Don't forget that a school's reputation may be quite out of date. The headmaster who built it up may have left, or the toughs who initially got it a bad name may now be parents themselves. Fee-paying parents often consult advisory bodies or scholastic agencies. These are useful in that they have access to a good deal of information and may have a note of vacancies, but they cannot make the choice for you. There really is no alternative to visiting the schools themselves. Many parents hesitate to do this, and some feel they have not got much out of the visit even when they do. The problem is partly one of unfamiliarity. Parents who have looked at schools for two or three of their children find it gets easier each time. But there is also a problem of over-familiarity, of the wrong sort. When you enter a school as a parent, very often for the first time since you were yourself at school, all the old feelings tend to stir again. You may have had a very happy time at school, but you were nonetheless a very junior person: the head teacher was very much the boss. It is quite hard, in these circumstances, to regard the head as a mere equal. Many parents allow themselves to be intimidated by a head who would be much less impressive if they met him casually. What is more, he is likely to be highly practised at dealing with parents, whereas you might not be at all used to dealing with head teachers.

Start with your nearest school. This is the normal place for a child to go, especially if he is just starting at five. If it does not seem satisfactory (the buildings may be a slum, the head a tyrant, the other pupils unacceptable) you can begin to look elsewhere. The first experience will be good practice. The cardinal rule in these visits is to begin with the child. This may sound obvious, but many parents ignore it. Fathers who put their son's name down at birth are an extreme example, but many parents have all sorts of ideas about what they require from a school which are only remotely connected to their child's needs. Once you have got as realistic a view as you can of these needs, make a list of the things you consider most important in a school with them in mind.

Of course, you will not find a school that is ideal in every respect. Each will have advantages and disadvantages, and you will have to balance one against the other. You may have to sacrifice some desirable need lower down your list for something that you consider more important, nearer the top. For example, on every parent's list there will probably be something about new and bright buildings, and there is no doubt that, other things being equal, a pleasant building surrounded with playing fields is an attraction. But it is quite possible to get a good education in a gaunt building, as some of our older public schools would no doubt agree. What is important is what the school is doing with its buildings. The most unpromising place can be made to look inviting, with exhibitions of the children's work and so on. You may well find yourself in the end choosing an elderly school because of its very progressive methods, or because it belongs to your religious denomination.

Another thing to look out for is overcrowding. In primary schools, classes of over forty are still found – and under twenty a stroke of luck, though you might find this in early days of a new school. The evidence about the effect of class sizes on the educational achievements of pupils is not conclusive, though common sense suggests that the fewer children a teacher has the more attention she will be able to give to each of them. Often, of course, the schools with the best reputations become the most overcrowded.

Some parents feel strongly about the other pupils in the school: they may hope that good manners will rub off on their own children, or fear that bad accents may be contagious. Both are no doubt true, but only you can decide how much it matters. I myself have a prejudice in favour of schools whose social mixture is similar to that of the whole population, with the children of professional people mixed up with those of skilled and unskilled manual workers, but many schools reflect their immediate neighbourhood and may be virtually one-class. What many teachers tend to say is that it is the home background that will win in the end, for good or ill, so it may not matter all that much if your delicate son is swearing like a trooper at eight.

The most important fact about a school is its staff. In most primary schools you can expect most of the staff to be trained, and you will want to concentrate on such things as the speed with which they leave the school. It is especially upsetting to the very young if their teachers change too rapidly. Some schools find it helpful if the first classes are taken by older married women: the girls straight from college are only too likely to get married and leave to have their own children. It is best, too, if the staff is fairly varied, with older and younger members and including both men and women. In secondary schools your demands of the teaching staff will be more complicated, and will be bound up with the range of work which the school offers. Try to get some idea, from a school prospectus or education office handout, of what sort of qualifications the staff have. Teachers will insist, though, that the possession of impressive degrees by no means guarantees an ability to teach.

Many parents feel that the kind of regime and atmosphere at a school is the most important thing about it. The starkest contrast is between, say, the primary school which 'streams' children by ability from the age of six or seven and concentrates on notching up proud numbers of eleven plus passes and that which lets children proceed at their own pace in groups of mixed ability where they are sociable rather than competitive beings. You may have strong views about this, but try to see that they relate to the child in front of you. For instance, you may feel desperately that eleven plus success is vital – and thus put into a formal forcing-house a child who would blossom in a much freer atmosphere.

Upon the kind of atmosphere which a school tries to create depends the kind of punishment it uses. One cannot be dogmatic about this, but I am now of the view that there is something wrong with any primary school which canes children. The question is a trifle more complicated in secondary schools, especially those with real disciplinary problems, and in the end teachers will have to manage as best they can. But if a secondary school canes at all regularly this tells you something about it – which you may like or not as the case may be.

A good secondary school has hosts of out-of-door activities going on: not only games but all sorts of clubs and societies, for debating, music, dramatics, archaeology, art, science and so on. Ask what sort of thing the school of your choice has: it will give you a good clue to the liveliness and energy of the staff.

Two questions which are of more importance, usually, to parents than to children are coeducational and religion. On the former there is evidence that coeducational schools are happier for staff and pupils and that the happiness is not at the expense of academic progress. On the latter, serious humanists will be puzzled to discover that they cannot send their children to a non-religious school. All schools have by law to offer religious instruction and a corporate act of worship. You can withdraw your child from both, but the school has to offer them.

These, then, are some of the things that you will want to be thinking about when you go to see the head teacher of a school. Try to visit him during school hours, and get him to show you round. You may get quite a good idea of the kind of school it is and the relations between the staff and pupils. Notice what the head considers most important: that can often be revealing. But the things I have been suggesting are examples only. You will have things that seem most important to you. But remember that in choosing a school you are balancing advantages and disadvantages: you may choose a traditional school in an old building because it gets good G.C.E. results; you may accept slum buildings because the school is so good at music; you may choose a convent, even though you yourself are a Methodist, because 'it gets such a nice type of child'.

This kind of balance is very difficult to keep in mind. When looking for a school parents often seize on one criterion and neglect others. One ought to be a bit suspicious of such single-mindedness: the individual child, remember, is very much more of a mixture. I have often seen parents expending enormous energy on getting their child into a school with a good academic record only to condemn him to five or seven years of relative misery and perhaps, on that account, to an unsatisfactory academic achievement. I have known 'progressive' parents meekly contemplating boarding schools (of which they disapprove) in order to find a school which has escaped 'the tyranny of exams'. It is as well to remember that one can't have everything. By concentrating on one thing, you may miss a great deal.

An extreme example of this is of the parent who is anxious for his child to go to the 'best' local school – whether this is the comprehensive with a high reputation or a local direct grant or independent school. This seems such a natural proceeding (everyone wants the best for his child) that it is worth throwing a doubt or two in the way. In the first place the reputations of schools may bear little relation to their performance. A school which has been good may be in a trough and one which has been bad may have pulled itself together. What is more, the reputation may be based on excellence at things you yourself do not much value. Even more important, even the best schools may not be very good for your particular child. But to my mind the chief disadvantage of the 'best' school is that it offers so little for the child to do. There is something rather dispiriting to many children in being required only to live up to, or to continue, an established reputation. In this sense, the up-and-coming school may offer more scope, more excitement and a better education. This is one reason why new schools are good places to be in, quite apart from the advantage of a new building. Some of the advantages of creating something new can also be gained in a school where the head and his staff are seeking change and experiment. Parents may often discover that it is the school without a heavy reputation which offers their children more scope for initiative and success and through that a better education.

But is there no school that you ought to move mountains to avoid? Perhaps in most areas there is one school with a very bad reputation which parents fear and shun. What if that is your local school? I do not myself believe that even this need be disastrous, though many parents feel it clearly is. Before despairing, however, check the reputation: discover what exactly is meant to be wrong. Visit the school: you will probably find that it is perfectly well equipped, though the buildings may be old. You may even find that it has a very good staff–student ratio, precisely because of its difficulties. Face the fact that you and other parents may have to work harder, to support your children at school and to support the school itself, but make sure that the basic provision is adequate. Try to judge the attitude of the head and his staff. It is hard to argue that you should willingly accept a school which is demoralized and hopeless (and I believe that local education authorities should not allow such schools to exist). But do not jump to conclusions. My wife recently found, in visiting local schools, that the liveliest impression was made by the school with by far the worst reputation.

A few parents pay fees for their children's education. They may do this reluctantly, because they cannot find what they want among local authority schools or because they want some form of special attention. They may do it because their family has always done it and the alternative does not occur to them. This is becoming less and less common at the primary stage. They may do it, as it were, determinedly, because of the advantages they see in private education. What they are buying, probably, is smaller classes, social advantage, a more formal educational atmosphere and middle-class chums for their children. They may want and get boarding school education. At the primary stage the teachers will be less well trained and the curriculum narrower than in the local schools. In secondary schools there may not be much in it. What they are not buying, it seems, is academic advantage. It looks as if children of comparable intelligence from similar social backgrounds do as well, or better, at O and A level in the local authority schools as in fee-paying schools. Anyway, you pays your money (in rates and taxes, and in fees) and you takes your choice.

4 Starting School

The first day at school is a big one in the lives of most children, and for some mothers too. Growth and development are, of course, continuous: a child does not suddenly become ready for school on his fifth birthday (or at any other time), but going to school dramatically marks the difference between infancy and childhood. Five-year-old children are normally ready for a wider social life than the family provides. They spend a good deal of time playing with others and form firm individual friendships with other children. They enjoy independence from adults. But the age of five for starting school compulsorily is quite arbitrary. Britain is one of the few countries in the world where this is the age. Most start compulsory education at six and a few as late as seven.

I am tempted to say that the first day at school is a problem for mothers rather than children. They view it with mixed feelings. On the one hand, it does represent the first move of the child away from them; on the other it is a proud part of his growing into independence. Those mothers in whom the former feeling overwhelmingly predominates will be most likely to have a difficult time themselves and with their children. What happens on the first day depends on the way a child has been brought up in the preceding years. If he has been encouraged to be outgoing and independent on a basis of secure affection, he will take to school with comparative ease. If his home has been insecure or if he has been over-protected, he may balk at it. There is, in other words, a good deal that parents can do to make the transition to school easy, but it is done in the whole process of upbringing. There is no magic system that will otherwise make it go all right on the day.

In dealing with the new school, the larger world, a child needs a sense of independence and the ability to manage on his own. What seem little things help, like being able to dress himself and tie his tie and shoe-laces. Some of these everyday skills take an awful long time to learn and busy mothers find it easier to do it themselves. But after the age of four, that temptation should be resisted and independence encouraged. Of course, the job will rarely be done perfectly. A tie will look as if it has been chewed into place; some children always seem to have a trailing shoe-lace; others have a tendency to flapping shirt-tails or droopy drawers. Never mind. And if a child really cannot get his fingers round a knot, let him wear shoes with buckles for school.

But independence comes in other ways too. The most obvious is in asking questions. I mentioned earlier the importance of language, and a child who is used to asking questions and getting answers is not only gaining a vocabulary. He is getting to grips with the world around him : the world becomes a place he can understand and master. One professor at London University, Basil Bernstein, has written about the different ways in which people speak and the different views of the world which are implied. Here is an example. The scene is on a bus : mother is sitting down and her child is standing by her. The bus is about to move off.

FIRST MOTHER: Hold tight.
CHILD: Why?
MOTHER: Hold *tight*.
CHILD: Why Mum?
MOTHER: Hold tight, I tell you, or I'll give you what for.

SECOND MOTHER: Hold tight.
CHILD: Why?
MOTHER: Because the bus is going to start and if you don't hold tight you'll fall over.

CHILD: Why Mum?
MOTHER: Well, you remember the other day when you were playing with your trolley and Johnny pulled it and you fell off . . .
CHILD: But why did I fall off?
MOTHER: Hold tight. And we'll ask Daddy when we get home.

The first child is getting a view of the world as an entirely arbitrary place, where things happen that he does not understand and which indeed cannot be understood. The second child may not always get a satisfactory answer, but at least he gets the impression that there are answers and that these can be discovered. The second child is well on the way to educating himself. Showing a normal interest, encouraging curiosity and answering questions are ways in which parents reinforce their children's urge to learn. It can often seem tedious and pointless, but if you can avoid ignoring or squashing the child, so much the better.

Some parents wonder whether to teach their children to read before school. Ambitious ones determine to do so. An obvious danger is that you might not get far enough to establish the skill thoroughly – so that the child may arrive at school only to be confused by a different method of learning and thus hindered rather than helped. Another difficulty is that parents get too emotionally involved with their children's learning, making the process a misery all round. On the other hand, if your child wants to know what the captions are on the television or begins to form letters when he is drawing or painting, there is no reason why you should not encourage him. Central to the capacity to read is the ability to distinguish different shapes and recognize like ones. There is a common puzzle in children's comics which involves picking the 'odd man out' from among four or five houses, dolls, sailing boats and so on. A child who can do this is (if you insist on instructional advantages) helping his ability to read. But systematic instruction at home is best avoided. When the child goes to school, of course, he may proudly tell you of the things which would have made you sweat blood to get into him at home.

It is helpful to remember that children are normally going to enjoy their infant school. You can honestly represent it as a treat and a privilege. Many mothers cannot face this: they see the school as taking the child away. And they may unconsciously give their children the idea that separation is a disaster, the school at best a necessary evil. They are not. Perhaps most children these days not only enjoy school when they get there but look forward to going. They may hear about it from older brothers and sisters. (With an only child you may have to arrange that the idea of school is familiar, by pointing out the school to him and, if you can, taking him to see it.) They recognize it as a step towards growing up, even if they would not put it like that. My daughter, at a small nursery school, often talked about the time she would go to the big boy's school. (As it happened she started at another which became 'my big school'.) You should encourage this anticipation now and again. There is no need to go on and on about it, but you can say how nice it will be to have lots of other children to play with, to have so many things to play with and to make and do. The point is, of course, that all children go to school, and this is in itself a comfort to the timid. The normality of the whole process can be an encouragement.

Some schools are beginning to be a help in this, and they are not always the schools in posh areas. One school I know invites parents to bring their children into the school occasionally during the year before they start. In this way they get used to the place. It holds no terrors for them, even though it is a tall nineteenth-century building. There is no such thing as admissions day at this school. Children are admitted individually. Five a day arrive with their mothers, and they go first to the headmistress's room. This is set out rather like a sitting-room, but one corner consists of shelves of books and toys where the child plays while the headmistress talks to mother and gets, incidentally, all the basic details about age and address and so on. The child is then introduced to his class teacher and she takes him along to join his class.

At the other extreme, it is still common to find primary schools admitting all the children, not only on the same day, but at the same moment. Mothers and children arrive at ten o'clock, and have been known to be required to queue in a corridor. Normally they may all wait in the school hall while one by one their names are read out, and labels hung round the children's necks saying 'Class I' or 'Class II'. No system is perfect, and even the most barbaric arrangements leave some children serene, but the cattle-dip method of entry very often means that it is common to see children being dragged kicking and screaming into the school during the following weeks. And this may have nothing to do with the actual lessons: it is just a reaction to that first awful day.

The Plowden Report suggested, as part of a minimum programme for relations between parents and schools, that a child and his parents need to be welcomed when he is first admitted to school (or when they have moved into a new district and he has to go to a new school). Each parent, it said, should be invited to see the head, to meet the class teacher, see at work the class into which his child would go and to visit and hear about the school and its organization. It felt that, unless the interview with the head was by appointment, it would not be leisurely enough.

I have already suggested that a number of schools fall far short of these suggestions, and the Report itself found that more than a third of parents did not see the head before their children started school. Under half of the children in a special starters survey visited their class before admission. You will see that the reception you and your child might get varies enormously from school to school. The important thing is to make the most of whatever is offered. One can get a very long way simply by assuming that what you want to do is normal. In a school which has a reputation of keeping parents at arm's length, one mother simply rang up and made an appointment with the head. As the interview drew to a close she said (rather than asked), 'May I go down to the reception class now?' and went.

My own experience has been that teachers and heads who are not immediately forthcoming are shy or uncertain rather than hostile. Brought up, sometimes, in a different tradition, they may be wary of taking the first step. Their fear of what havoc the bossy parent might wreak is no less real for being a fear of the unknown. In these circumstances a courteous approach is normally entirely successful. In most cases there is no need to go looking for trouble. On the other hand, I have heard of behaviour by head teachers that can be explained only in terms of ignorant stubbornness. You may be unlucky.

However gentle and well-organized the introduction to school may be, both you and your child will have the odd difficulty. Partly this will be a matter of adjusting to the new circumstances. He will be coping with perhaps forty other children for six hours a day. He will be in a new society whose rules he must learn. He has a life which is quite separate from yours. You, if you are the mother of an only child, may suddenly feel that life is empty. Most mothers feel a bit put out when their children first leave. All these feelings and difficulties are entirely normal. Even children who looked forward to going to school, and do so happily for a few days or a week, sometimes balk at it soon afterwards. The best thing here is to be gentle but firm: say that all children go to school now that they are five. Some children become more cheeky after a few days at school; others take to beating up their smaller brothers and sisters. This is what you would expect from the intense mixture of pride, fright and jealousy which they must be experiencing. Some children become very irritable. Often this is due to tiredness: a child may put a bold face on it while actually at school, but afterwards he may grizzle and even cry. The right thing is to get him to bed, but he will more than likely resist going. Suggest he goes and sits on his bed, playing with his toys, but that he need not go to sleep. You are just as likely to find him gratefully asleep within minutes. If the tiredness goes on for more than a few weeks have a word with his teacher. Sometimes schools will agree to take children half time only at this age (though this is in fact breaking the law).

One change which some mothers find hard to take is the child's affection for his teacher. He may come home full of what Miss X did, and of what Miss X knows. He may correct you in something, quoting Miss X as evidence. Sweet reasonableness is your appropriate response (as it will be when he brings his first dreadful girl friends home ten years later). On the other hand, some children improve visibly on going to school: they become more responsible and willing to help, less irritable and more controlled. Mothers may become reconciled sooner than they think to the absence of their children at school. There are compensations.

5 The Pattern of Learning

Going into a modern primary school is often a bewildering experience for parents. Gone are the rows of desks all facing the blackboard that were the mark of the traditional school. The children may be milling about in a way that looks very much like chaos. Parents wonder sometimes how the teacher can stand it.

A good way of understanding what is going on is to visit a classroom, if you can, twice, once when the children are absent and once when they are there. When the room is empty you can see that it is composed of a lot of different areas of work. One corner may be in effect a library, with shelves along the walls and a few tables and chairs. One class I went into had a carpet on the 'library' floor to help the effect of quietness and something special. Near the window, or perhaps near a door leading directly onto the playground, there may be a 'nature table' with plants growing – not just mustard and cress or peas in a jar, but flowers and small trees. The table is likely to be full of twigs and other objects the children have brought to school. There may be a hamster or rabbit in a cage. Both of these features, the library and the nature table, may strike parents as educational. But what about the school 'shop' or 'flat'? They may look too much like 'play'. So might the paints, clay and so on. You may even see, not only proper musical instruments, but made-up ones consisting of bottles or jars filled with water, each of which gives out a different note when you hit it. The most unfamiliar area of all may be the 'number table' covered with coloured blocks and rods. Arithmetic was not like that when we were at school. And all round the walls there will be charts and drawings, self-portraits of the children, lessons about the weather, small experiments and accounts of visits.

Now visit the same class with the children in it. Once you have got used to the moving scene, look at individual children. You may be astonished to realize that each child is occupied, going about what he rightly calls his work. A few children may be reading or writing, others feeding or cleaning the hamster. Some may be making what you would regard as too much noise with some recorders. Some may be selling each other old cornflake packets in the shop or being mothers and fathers in the flat. There may be a good deal of weighing and measuring going on. A child may be standing against the wall while another marks off his height. You may also catch a glimpse of the teacher, moving about, watching, listening, suggesting, helping, and never in the way.

Not all schools are as free as the one I have just described, but more and more are becoming so, and there are very few indeed which are not touched by these methods in something that they do. And this whole enterprise has been described as 'probably the world's most ambitious pattern of beginning instruction'. That phrase may give us a clue to understand it: what goes on in primary schools is not a matter of chance or whim or sentimentality on the part of the teachers. It is based upon what we know of the way children grow and develop, and it is probably the first time ever that general education has been so based.

We have seen in Chapter 1 the main facts and principles of growth, and in Chapter 2 something of the importance of play. It is enough here to remember that children develop at different rates (indeed two children of five can be further apart in development than the average five-year-old from the average four-year-old). They progress in the same sequence of development but at different rates, and there may be critical periods when development can be significantly helped or hindered. Play is the principal means of learning in early childhood, whether of skills or in emotional and intellectual development. These ideas, so simply stated here, have evolved out of a good deal of intuition confirmed and tempered by research findings over many decades. Learning, like growth, comes through the interaction of the child with his environment; each experience changes (however slightly) the structure of the child's mind and contributes to his whole picture of the world.

It is now time to see how these ideas affect what actually goes on in schools, how they lead to the kind of classroom I described earlier on. The keynote is 'flexibility'. If children develop at different rates, then surely school work must be flexible, allowing each child to come to reading or writing, say, when he is ready for it. The idea that all the children in a class must get through a given amount of material in a certain length of time, and that those who do not have somehow failed, goes against all that is known about children. In the early 1930s a very few primary schools adopted what they called 'free play' for part of the day. Gradually this idea was extended, until now some schools feel confident enough to give almost the whole of the day to it. What it means in fact is that the children spend their time in activities which they themselves have chosen, from the wide variety which a good class teacher provides. Even those schools which limit the amount of 'play' tend to encourage an overlap between this and the more formal periods, so that reading and writing may grow out of the children's own interests.

Now this is all quite different from the old style timetable which was rigidly divided into specific periods for spelling, dictation, grammar, composition, recitation, reading, handwriting, tables and mental arithmetic. And, although it is quite certainly better for the children, it may leave their parents somewhat adrift.

This flexibility is not confined to the distribution of the

day: it extends to the curriculum. Instead of the 'subjects' we all remember, a class may embark upon a 'project' or a 'centre of interest' – say transport, or our town, birds or naval warfare. The topic may be chosen by the children themselves. The thing to notice about it is that it is likely to cover every 'subject' one can think of. The children will have to read books and look things up in encyclopedias, they will have to write, not only labels and captions, but short accounts of methods or events. They will be involved, without formally knowing it, in history, geography, science and all. They will almost certainly have to do a great deal of calculation. (Even the hamster gives rise to a great deal of arithmetic. Each week the children must decide how much food to get and how much it will cost, and a rota will be made to show when each child must clean out the cage.)

Some schools are even more flexible than this. The one I described earlier will have virtually no set periods at all, and almost no times when all the children will be doing the same things. The exceptions may be music, movement, poetry or stories, though even these may not always be taken in convenient groups. In all this the schools are trying to accommodate the wide variations in the needs of individual children.

A second main way in which the principles of growth affect the practice of the schools is in building upon the children's own experience. If children learn best through interaction with their environment, then this is what the school should provide. This applies both in the classroom itself and in the outside world. In the classroom teachers try to make it possible for children to discover things for themselves rather than simply keep telling them all the time. A child who discovers something for himself not only gets a great thrill out of it, he learns and retains it better. So primary school education involves fewer lectures and more practical work. Similarly, a lot of teachers try to let their lessons grow out of a child's own environment. The Plowden Report mentioned children doing 'traffic counts' or asking shopkeepers about sources of their goods The object is to see things in action, rather than hear about them in class – hence the growing numbers of school visits, to museums and galleries or to the countryside for urban children and to cities for rural ones. This means that learning can be based upon first-hand experience, which is the way children learn best.

All this will be seen perhaps more clearly in the next chapter, as we tackle the various 'subjects' of the primary school curriculum. But we need this overall view to set the stage, so to speak.

Before leaving this topic, I ought to meet the criticism of those parents who feel that, all right, the children are happier in modern schools and do a great variety of things, but is it really education? Parents often worry whether a child is being fitted for the world he will enter after leaving school where 'everything is not all play' and people have to do boring and uncongenial tasks. Will a child who has followed his own interests for so long be fitted to cope with a world which is not devoted to satisfying them? There are, I suppose, two answers to this. The first is that what goes on at school should not necessarily relate directly to later life: the best preparation for adulthood is to have lived fully as a child, not to have been limited to some supposed preparation for tedium. The second answer to the parent's worry is to point out that it assumes that the new methods are not concerned with the traditional virtues of neatness, accuracy, care, perseverance and the sheer accumulation of knowledge. All these things are important, but they were not automatically fostered by the old methods in education. Modern teachers would claim that their approach lays a firmer foundation for them than the old. And there is some evidence that the new methods are at any rate not setting the old skills back. The Department of Education and Science has for years carried out a survey of reading ability in schools. This has been steadily improving since the war, though the latest survey suggests that the improvement has levelled off.

But the best way to be convinced about the new primary schools is to visit them and talk to the teachers. It really is quite astonishing how the new methods have spread in the public education system in Britain, so that teaching is based upon a respect for the individual child that used to be confined to 'progressive' schools. The reason for this is that teachers have on the whole wanted it, have been trained for it and thus understand it. This revolution has come from inside: it has not been imposed upon schools by cranks and unrealistic inspectors. And if, after talking to a good primary school teacher, you still object to the new methods, ask yourself what it was in your own upbringing that made you so unresponsive to change.

6 The Primary School Curriculum

It is all very well to talk, as we have in the last chapter, about principles, methods and attitudes, but what do schools actually do? This chapter is about the curriculum of primary schools – and secondary schools will be dealt with in Chapter 8. In primary schools we have a difficulty which arises from the new method that the school day is not divided rigidly into separate periods. One activity flows into another, and there may well be times when different groups of children are doing quite different things. The younger the children are, the harder the task of dividing their activities by subjects, though by the end of primary school, at ten or eleven, the timetable will have its more familiar divisions. In this chapter, the work of the primary school is divided for convenience into three groups: basic subjects, sciences and social studies and the creative element.

Basic Subjects: English and Mathematics

The traditional task of the infants' school is to teach children to read, and it is worth saying at once that this is still so. Perhaps a quarter or a third of children have not mastered the skill entirely by the time they go to the junior school at eight, but this is recognized as a problem. English in the modern primary school has come to exemplify both the new methods themselves (it appears as an essential part of almost every subject of the curriculum) and also parental disquiet about their consequences. Some of the latter may have been set at rest by the knowledge, mentioned in the previous chapter, that standards of reading are on the whole improving. This chapter will go further and try to show what teachers are trying to do these days in English lessons.

Perhaps the clue to this is the recognition that the most fundamental step towards literacy is taken by children before they go to school. They learn to speak, and parents should not under-estimate either the size of this achievement in learning or their own contribution to it. What the new primary schools try to do in English is to develop fluency in speech and to build upon this a secure grasp of reading and writing. Part of the hubbub and chat which so surprises parents entering primary classes for the first time has this positive purpose. One reason why classes no longer sit patiently facing the front, responding at most to an occasional question-and-answer session, is that that kind of silence and order is very stultifying. The role of the teacher today is to move from one individual or group to another, talking to children, and, above all, listening to them. Gradually the children themselves build up not only an extensive vocabulary, which is the best basis for learning to read, but also the desire to record what they say, which is the best reason for learning to write.

This building up of a vocabulary is of enormous importance. Only now are we coming to understand fully the difficulties which stand in the way of children from poorly educated homes. One of them, certainly, is that the schools may try to teach them the mechanics of reading before they have any secure grasp of the spoken language. When this happens it can quickly lead to bewilderment, failure and demoralization.

So parents should not worry if they find primary classes in which there is a buzz of conversation. Of course, there are quite different kinds of noises, as any teacher knows, which indicate that a class is bored, out of hand, resentful or in a state of riot. But such indications are recognizable and comparatively rare. Parents will soon recognize the more purposeful sound that comes from a good primary school at work. It is not only children who find that problems are easier for having been able to talk about them, and this basically is what is going on. Of course, not all of the conversation will always be directly relevant. It would be surprising if a conversation about measurement did not on occasion stray to holidays or football, but there was no guarantee that children attended more consistently under the old methods, and a child's span of concentration can be very short. But parents may be comforted to know that conversation, any conversation, *contributes* to modern methods, whereas it would have destroyed the effect of the older ones. And in any case, the unobtrusive presence of a teacher who is moving amongst the children makes pure time-wasting much less likely.

Some teachers want to go further in their encouragement of children's speech. They try to see that children speak 'correctly'. There are dangers in this. In the first place it is not always clear what is correct in pronunciation, vocabulary and grammar. An attempt to get children to speak like the old B.B.C. is almost certainly doomed to failure, as is a too rigid insistence on the niceties of grammar. What is important is that children should be fluent and clear. You do not encourage them to use new words by despising the ones they have.

Reading and writing can arise naturally out of activity and speech. For example, a child may want to write his name on a piece of work or label a drawing: 'Mummy washing up' or 'My boat'. The teacher will write this down and the child will copy it. Useful words, which are needed by a number of children, will be written on the blackboard or pinned up on cards in various parts of the room. A lot of the room's features may themselves be labelled: the door will have 'door' pinned to it. All this means that the formal, systematic teaching of reading and writing is being introduced quite easily in the child's experience. School is not just a matter of chatting.

As you might expect, there are a number of reading

methods used by schools, and most teachers use more than one. A sensitive teacher will vary her methods to suit individual children and should encourage children to use all the ways they know in tackling particular puzzling words or phrases. There are perhaps two basic approaches. The first is an extension of those word cards pinned up round the room. In it the children memorize the look of whole words and phrases, often with the help of pictures. Not surprisingly this is often known as the 'look and say' method, and the word cards which teachers may hold up for the children to recognize are known as 'flash' cards. The point here is that children associate the sense of a word with its shape and they can quickly progress to phrases or sentences. There are a number of sets of books available in which pictures are connected by short phrases, to be varied only slightly from one page to another. For example, 'this puppy can see a frog'; 'this puppy can see a robin'; 'this puppy can see two mice'; 'these puppies can see a snail'; 'this kitten can see a spider'. Each of these sentences has an appropriate picture which makes the words fairly obvious. An extension of this method is to introduce new words in a context (often with a picture) where they can be reasonably guessed.

A second approach starts not from whole words but from the sounds of letters. This is often called the phonic or phonetic method. Its advantage is that it enables children to 'build up' long or unfamiliar words from their individual parts. The teacher often introduces this after children have mastered a number of words by the 'look and say' method, because 'look and say' can leave children with no way of reading words which they have never met before. But the phonic method has the disadvantage that English spelling can often be very eccentric. So it becomes quite hard to 'build up' the words, for example: rough, though, through, bought, plough, cough, borough. What teachers have to do is to give children as many ways as possible of tackling new words.

Needless to say there have been many attempts to get

round the unhelpfulness of English spelling. One, which has had some publicity lately, is an initial teaching alphabet (i.t.a.). This is in itself a method of teaching reading. As its name implies, it is a different alphabet from the one we normally use, and its 'letters' more closely reflect the sounds of English. In particular it has forty-four letters, each representing one sound only, instead of the normal twenty-six, and its authors claim that this removes much of the early difficulty created by English spelling. Perhaps one school in twenty today has used i.t.a., and many who have report enthusiastically about its effects. The obvious objection, that when they have learned to read from i.t.a. the children may have difficulty in transferring to the normal alphabet (or traditional orthography – t.o. – in the jargon), turns out to be unjustified. The switch is made, apparently, without fuss. But it is also fair to say that there is insufficient long-term experience of i.t.a. in general use to have convinced teachers that they should go over to it entirely.

A more radical development is *Words in Colour*, in which, briefly, each sound is illustrated by a particular colour, regardless of the way in which it is spelled. Reading in black and white is carried on simultaneously and colour is used very much as a clue. The fully developed theory of words in colour is based upon the educational ideas of its author, Dr Caleb Gattegno.

Whatever the methods used for learning to read, the modern primary school is not likely to rely purely upon formal instruction. One of its characteristics is the greatly improved provision of books of all kinds. Though, of course, teachers will claim (rightly) that the book allowance is never good enough, it is now entirely common for primary school classrooms to have their own 'library corner' where books, whether of stories, poetry, information or entertainment, are always available. In many cases it is made a point of calm amid the busy life of the class. The school is likely to have a library too, and there may be periods set aside during the week for the class to go there to borrow books. This gives the children a wider choice: the school library can be very much bigger and better than a class library. This library provision means that, almost without knowing it, the children become used to handling books. They turn to books naturally for fun and facts. They get practice in reading and almost instinctively come to understand that the skill of reading is a way of mastering a subject, enlarging experience and extending enjoyment.

The upshot of all this is that parents are unlikely to find their children beginning reading and writing by learning the names of letters or reciting the alphabet. What is it that they learn, after all, when they know that 'h' is called aitch? Nor will they find themselves helping in long practised lines of i, u, v, w. The precise curl of the letter g will not loom large in modern education. Of course, a number of parents will object that writing in particular remains pretty scruffy for too long. Surely, they feel, children should be encouraged to be neat, to form their letters correctly, and so on. Even those who do not regret the passing of copperplate may yet hanker for a little more regularity.

Here too there has been a certain amount of thought in the school. The old demands for good writing did, after all, eat up a great deal of time which might have been better spent. The crucial discovery was that a neat hand with broad downstrokes and narrow upstrokes requires more muscular control than young children are consistently capable of. Many schools, therefore, have gone over to what is known as italic script, in which the shape of the nib makes the strokes thick or thin according to the direction in which it is being moved. Its advocates claim that it is more elegant and legible, just as quick and (most important) better able to keep its standard over long periods of writing at speed.

Another worry that parents have is that children do not have lessons in 'grammar'. Employers and people who write to the newspapers may complain that young people do not know their parts of speech. But the fact is that we learn to speak and write well by reading and writing a lot and by doing so with awareness and care. If we want to discuss the use of words we may have to know the names of the various parts of speech, for quick reference. So a primary school child may know that a noun is a naming word, a verb is a doing word and so on, but he is unlikely to be fascinated by different categories of adjectival clauses. English is an irregular language and attempting to teach grammar can often be a wearisome trudge through innumerable exceptions to rather unnatural general rules. There are naturally some people who want to study the grammar or structure of language – a study which is illuminating language and literature on the one hand and the psychology of learning on the other – but they are not on the whole seven or eight years old. In short, grammar was one of the essential parts of the old school curriculum which was almost universally forgotten as soon as school was left behind.

It is probably true to say that most parents are pleased by the development of newer methods in English, as in other subjects in the primary school. Those unconvinced are puzzled rather than hostile. But even when convinced by the new methods, parents may still be puzzled about what it all means for them. In the old days it was fairly easy for parents to hear a child recite the alphabet, or practise letters, or stumble through 'C – A – T : cat'. Parents still want to help, but if the methods are different from those they remember they may hesitate to intervene. This in its turn may make them a little resentful of the school, even when they can see that the new methods suit their children and produce results. On the other hand, many parents think they want to help more than they actually do. What they are really asking for is a chance to understand what is happening and to be in a position to encourage and support at moments when the need for it crops up. They are asking about the new methods, not in order to conduct their own continuous programme of educational extension lectures, but so that in a much vaguer sense they can feel on the same side as the children and the schools.

As far as English is concerned, the new methods themselves give us a clue as to what kind of support and help parents can give with reading and writing. There are, of course, still some teachers who wonder whether parents can help at all – apart from a general preparation for school and in making the home a place which encourages learning. Most children, after all, do master the basic skills of reading and writing before they leave the infant school, which means that they do so earlier than children almost anywhere else in the world – so there is normally little reason to intervene. Indeed, perhaps the best advice that one can give to parents at this stage is, relax. Remember that you too are learning, perhaps for the first time, all about the way children cope with schools. If, for example, you are tempted to feel that your child is behind in some way, then by all means have a word with the teacher. But remember too that children do develop at different rates and should normally be left to do so. (There has been a difference of literally years between the ages at which my own children, for example, learned to read.) Remember too, that if you are getting anxious about your child's progress you are not in the best position to help him. The emotional relationship between parent and child may inhibit learning at the best of times: if you are over-anxious as well, you may easily do more harm than good. Similarly, the variety of methods of learning to read and write may mean that you are in some difficulty about where to begin. At best your efforts may be met with scorn: 'No, we don't do it that way.' At worst you may badly confuse the child.

Still it must be admitted that teachers are not altogether consistent about this. They may urge parents not to worry; to let the child develop at his own pace; to avoid coaching and similar pressures. But, at the same time, they may stream children according to their ability, and they do this normally in the primary school by progress in reading, writing and arithmetic. This means that a child's ability to read at some stage may seriously affect his whole educational experience and opportunities in life. There is no way of judging whether a child who is reading poorly is developing at an average rate towards something under average ability, or is developing slowly towards real talent. A child may have real difficulty with reading and thus be streamed with children working much below his capacity in other things, like mathematics. So if teachers make performance important, they should not be surprised if parents try to improve it. This sort of pressure of both parents and teachers will continue to exist certainly as long as there is selection at eleven.

Even so, in normal circumstances, most teachers would advise parents to give background help rather than to attempt direct instruction in reading, and this is almost certainly right. We have already seen the importance of talking to children, of explaining what one is doing during the routine of daily life. Remember that much of it is new to the children even when it has become drudgery to oneself. If it helps to think of this sort of conversation as something formal, like enlarging vocabulary, then by all means do so. It is what you are actually doing, after all. Be ready, too, with constructive praise. If a child does read or write at home, this is very much more important than trying to see that children get things right. The day your child comes to you with his name written on a piece of paper with half of the letters the wrong way round is a day for an exclamation of joy, not a pedantic concern for accuracy. Children will want, after all, to practise the new skills they have learned at school, so one of the things you can do is to find ways of letting them. Let them write out invitation cards to birthday parties (taking care only to see that they are not entirely incomprehensible). Encourage letters to friends and relations – and not only those 'thank you' letters which can make any gift a bore. Let them write out and stick up on their bedroom door notices saying 'prvit', 'no entry', 'prise 1 peny', 'plese nock'. There are many situations at home where children can naturally be asked to write: shopping lists, for example, or a note for the milkman.

One of the things that surprises parents is the length of time that it takes for a skill like writing to become established. Parents sometimes lose patience or even despair. A child who for six months will spell 'deb' for 'bed' may look to some anxious parent like a bundle of psychological, emotional and educational difficulties. In fact he is entirely normal. There are some children who do need special help with their particular difficulties, and these are discussed in Chapter 11, but the thing to remember is that most children don't. Most of their problems in fact solve themselves, and this is true of most of the difficulties children may have with writing. Parental support for early attempts at reading should be similar to that for writing. It is, of course, a help if there are books in the house, especially if parents are occasionally seen reading them. But books are not the only possibility. You need not despise comics, or strip cartoons of popular papers. Some of these are very much better than some early reading books. The pictures are more vivid and clear, the story they tell more interesting – and they fit the action to the captions with greater skill. There may be objections to some comics on moral grounds (some parents may regard brutality and lust as less than ideal for seven-year-olds), but there are not many educational objections, especially at the primary school stage. The main point is that children should be reading and enjoying what they read and some comics are admirable for this purpose. Parents can shop around and find the ones they consider the most suitable.

But there is no need to stop at comics. It can be a great help if you can manage to buy books that the children can regard as their own; and if there can be a special place or shelf on which they can keep them. Try not to worry too much if the first books tend to get scribbled in and pulled about. This is inevitable and they will stop doing it quite soon.

There may even come a time when they start looking after them.

Let the children join the local library as well. They can choose books for themselves by the time they are of school age. Perhaps you yourself are in the habit of reading to your children. Lots of parents do. Others find it an intolerable bore. One solution for the latter is to wheel in grandparents and other relations or friends for whom it is a joy.

Some schools also give parents some guidance by compiling lists of books suitable for various ages. Others may suggest more formal series of readers different from those that the children read at school. This is sensible because parents who present their children with the same material as the school very often find that the response is one of yawning indifference.

If parents are puzzled by some of the new methods of teaching English, they are often at a complete loss when faced with the new mathematics. The revolution in methods here is even more recent, and children are likely to be tackling things which are totally unfamiliar to their parents. You may remember learning the four arithmetic processes of addition, subtraction, multiplication and division, and applying these not only to 'whole numbers' but to fractions, decimals, money, feet and inches and so on. You may recall the ritual chanting of multiplication tables and an emphasis on 'quick and accurate mental arithmetic'. Now, for all you can gather from your children, modern mathematics may seem to be no more than fiddling with coloured blocks. What, you may ask, has happened?

It is worth wondering why the new methods have spread so quickly. Teachers are not naturally a particularly revolutionary profession. Change comes slowly in schools as a rule. Reformers often complain about the difficulty of securing change. This is partly because individual teachers are to a certain extent isolated in their own classrooms; there are no national directives about the curricula and methods to be used. Even reforming head teachers have to carry their staff's voluntary agreement to change. This means that a new idea has to be accepted by each individual teacher before it can become generally accepted. And teachers pride themselves on being practical people, relying more upon their own experience and knowledge of the children than on theories from outside. In these circumstances, it is clear that, if new methods spread quickly, it is because teachers are generally dissatisfied with the old ones and are on the look out for improvement.

This was especially true of the older attitudes to mathematics. These relied heavily on the purely mechanical operation of skills and formulae – and it was generally thought that, until children had mastered these basic skills and could apply them, there was no point in trying anything more adventurous and interesting. Hence the endless examples of simple additions involving carrying 10 and the like. There were several things wrong with this. In the first place many children actually got nowhere at all. Despite all the practice, they never mastered the mechanical skills of addition, subtraction and so on. The standard of mathematical competence among most children was deplorably low. At the same time mathematics became not only a subject in which most people failed, but also one which was extremely boring. Page after page of the same sums every day, week after week, and indeed year after year, became an unproductive misery. Even worse in some ways was the fact that a number of relatively bright children managed to master the skills, to get high marks and pass examinations without ever understanding what mathematics were about. If there are many adults today whose hatred and suspicion of figures is based upon failure in mathematics at school, there are others whose hatred and suspicion is based upon their spurious success.

So the basis of the new methods was a questioning of the old ones. Teachers began asking themselves what was the value of learning by rote? What have you gained, when you have learned the 4 times table? But it was not enough simply to be dissatisfied. If you want to scrap the old method, you have to have something to put in its place. What teachers did was to go back to what is known about the ways children grow and develop on the one hand and to the nature and development of mathematics on the other.

The point about children learning is that they grasp mathematical ideas much more slowly than people used to think and that they learn best through their own experience and through their own activities. Let us take a simple example. It seems entirely obvious to parents that a pint is a pint, whether it is in a tapering bottle, a fat jug or a shallow pan. The fact is that we have all had to learn this. It is not at once obvious to young children. So you will often see in a primary school children having a splendid time sloshing water in and out of glass containers of various shapes and sizes. You may think that this is all simply play and messing about, but until a child knows from his own experience that a pint is a pint whatever its shape, there is not much sense in giving him sums to do about pints. This principle extends throughout mathematics. A circle is a circle whatever its size – and circles have properties in common. For example, the distance around the edge always has the same relationship to the widest distance across the middle (or, as they say in jargon, the circumference is equal to the diameter x π). It is clear, then, how the teaching of mathematics should be approached. First, the children should start with the facts of the world around them; then they should begin to understand relationships; and only when these are well understood should they practise the use of the concept involved. Practice must follow understanding and not be independent as it was in the old days.

To a lot of people this is all too simple for words. Can it really be necessary, they ask, to spend so much time establishing elementary ideas like more or less? longer and shorter? bigger and smaller? Does there have to be quite so much weighing and measuring? Are all those cards and counters, coloured rods and balls, bottles and cans really education?

Can't children perfectly well play at shops in the holidays? The answers to those questions and others like them is that this sort of approach really does seem like a basis for improved mathematical understanding. But it is more than that. When children understand what it is they are doing they become capable of things which were previously thought beyond the grasp of most children even in the secondary school. For example, all that weighing and measuring leads to writing down records, and children can be encouraged to express these records in such devices as graphs. Before you know where they are, primary school children can manage elementary statistics. If children come to use symbols on the basis of understanding what the symbols refer to, even the dreaded division sign is literally child's play and ten-year-olds happily tackle elementary symbolic logic. Geometry, algebra and trigonometry (though few teachers are daft enough to use these names) are a common feature of primary education, when only a few years ago they were thought to be suitable for grammar school children only. In other words, by respecting the speed at which children come to understand mathematical ideas, teachers in today's primary schools can lead them to interests and achievements which are far in advance of previous practice.

The new methods in mathematics have one temporary consequence: they make it even harder for parents to give children direct help. It is common today for parents to be less good at mathematics at any level than their infant children. But this need not be a disadvantage. You can always turn your child's scorn and derision at your own inadequacies to some purpose. Let him boast and show off. Let him, in short, teach you mathematics. One of the difficulties conscientious parents have is that their interested questions about school work are often brushed impatiently aside. Mothers often say that they can never get their children to tell them anything about what goes on at school. Where the direct approach fails, a well-timed demonstration of genuine ignorance may succeed. If a rather lordly explanation begins, try not to be put off by the unfortunate manner of your seven-year-old lecturer and do try to pay attention. Try not to feel on the defensive. Don't keep implying that the school ought to be doing something else or something different, and try not to keep exclaiming at what you regard as gaps in the children's knowledge. Try to understand instead the extent of what they actually know. A heavily censorious view of the frivolity of modern mathematics may ill become those of us whose own mathematical foundations are none too firm. The children will find us out in the end.

On the other hand, there are some parents who feel so strongly committed to the multiplication tables that they are unhappy unless their children know them. If your child does not seem to be learning these at school, and you feel he ought, it may be that you should teach him. But it is as well to remember that you are probably embarking upon this more for your own peace of mind than for his education. You ought probably to have a word with his teacher first, just to make sure that there is no serious danger of spreading confusion, and do not be surprised if the only visible result of your efforts is that your child prefers mathematics at school to mathematics at home.

There are plenty of other things that you can more reasonably and productively do. There are innumerable natural opportunities at home for the basic experiences of mathematics: for comparing, measuring, counting and calculating. If you can bear the burden of being 'helped' by your children while shopping, cooking, dressmaking, gardening or woodworking, you can give them plenty of practice in mathematics. But do be ready for the conflicting surprises that children may take longer than you expect grasping some things and will be capable of more than you imagine in others.

Science and Social Sciences

There is much more to primary education these days than reading, writing and arithmetic and, although the change may not be so great everywhere as it is in mathematics, it is fair to say that every part of the curriculum is being revised and re-thought, often very rapidly. As Chapter 5 made clear, it is often hard to have separate 'subjects' in primary schools because one topic will flow into another or one particular project may cover so many different subjects. A project on the school's neighbourhood may employ what would be recognized as English, geography, history and art. A centre of interest like 'sound' may explore physics, mathematics and music. But for convenience and because parents may still remember the old subjects, this part of the chapter will be devoted to science and those subjects like history and geography which are coming to be called social studies.

To take the latter first, children enjoy history. Authors relentlessly write historical novels for them. History is romance, adventure, escape to a different world – and it is all true. Present-day practice in primary schools recognizes this appeal. Children are less often bound to a textbook. Few are set to memorize dates or the sequence of the kings and queens of England. One reason for this is that children do not develop a sense of time until the later years of primary school, if then. The date of, say, 1666 is meaningless to them. Instead, teachers may approach history in two ways. The first may start from what is familiar – like the children's own neighbourhood or town – and then delve into the past to show how it came to be what it is today. The children may emerge from this with a fairly sketchy idea of the length of time involved, but at least they will have some sense of the continuity of human experience and their own roots in the past. The second approach is to plunge directly into a different time and place, emphasizing the difference between then and now. Here it is precisely the remoteness of the experience (of the Great Fire of London or the defeat of the Spanish Armada) which is attractive to the children, and which introduces them to the variety of human achievement and the richness of the modern heritage.

Whatever the approach, however, the children are unlikely to get it out of textbooks, or from copying down notes. In the first place, they are likely to be asked to discover the facts by searching through books in the class or school library, and they will write up their discoveries not only in their own notebooks but in great folders to which the whole class contributes. They are likely to act out historical scenes, and write their own stories of the 'I was there' kind. They may make models of medieval villages, Elizabethan men of war or of eighteenth-century towns.

The same pattern may be seen in geography. The traditional rhyme said that history was about chaps and geography about maps. But few children nowadays learn by heart such things as the names of the capes and bays around the coast of Britain. Again the approach may be either through a study of the neighbourhood, widening to include the nation and the world, or through exotic places with bizarre climates. And geography is about chaps too: many of the books in the class library tell about life as it is lived by people in different parts of the world. The lessons may arise from the children's own experience or from visits. The latter lead to descriptive writing and to maps and charts. Perhaps most classrooms keep a careful daily note of the weather and compare other more extreme climates with their own experience, systematically recorded. Others trace the origins of everyday foods and fabrics. Others take topics like transport by land, sea or air. It is obvious that with this approach geography and history can be inextricably intertwined. Some schools go even further and learn about the early life of their neighbourhood in ways which are recognizably derived from sociology. They answer such questions as: where do people live? what work do they do? where are their amusements and entertainments? what sort of schools are provided? and so on.

When most parents were at primary school science consisted largely of 'nature study': classrooms tended to be filled with catkins in the spring and fallen leaves in the autumn. And certainly the most useful way of introducing young children to science is through the study of living things. Today's classrooms are full of plants: you may find a tiny oak growing in a bottle, its root system revealed, and there may be a profusion of boxes of this and pots of that. Animals, too, are increasingly common: guinea pigs, hamsters and rabbits all have their place alongside the more traditional frogspawn. These pets are not just sentimental or decorative. You will find the minutest care with their feeding and cleaning arrangements, together with an elaborate system of recording their consumption and habits, but primary school science is also rapidly widening its scope. Children always enjoy magnets, models, syphons, pulleys, levers and magnifying glasses, and you can expect to find these in the classrooms. But nowadays, a good deal of the more systematic teaching, which used to be left to the secondary school, is being introduced to help children understand their physical surroundings. Railway-engines, motor cars, television, aeroplanes and telescopes are all possible, even likely topics for primary school study.

As with other subjects, the children often begin with an investigation on the basis of their own experience. But in this way they are often introduced early to the methods of science. They learn to observe carefully and to record accurately. They discover the importance of asking the right questions and of knowing where to begin finding the answers. Most important, they learn the basic lesson of science, which is that one should not simply jump to conclusions: these have to be carefully checked. One basis of science – the checking of hypotheses – becomes familiar to children in their primary school.

Many schools find that in the study of living things questions naturally arise about human beings – including questions about sex. Many teachers today are unabashed by the subject, but most still treat it rather gingerly. They feel it is properly the concern of parents. This is because it is not simply a question of the physical facts: human sex includes love and an understanding of personal relationships. On the other hand, not all parents are ready to accept responsibility here, and it is probably true to say that very few are ready to do so early enough. Many normal girls, and increasing numbers of them, have their first menstrual period while at primary school, so they need to know what is going on at that stage. The schools have a duty towards those children whose parents have left them inadequately prepared, and even the Education Act of 1944 has been held to imply that local authorities must provide sex education to fulfil the duty placed upon them to contribute to the moral development of the community.

So increasing numbers of primary schools are offering systematic sex education. If the school does so the head teacher is likely to write to parents telling them what is planned and giving them the chance to withdraw their children from the lessons. Some take more trouble than this, holding meetings at which the proposals are explained. Most parents are normally pleased and a bit relieved when the school takes an initiative of this kind, so there is seldom any difficulty, but every now and again a parent may feel quite strongly that it is wrong to give sex education in a classroom. He may feel that it is making public something which is essentially private. If you have hesitations of this kind, quell them. Determining that your child shall be the only one leaving the room when sex is discussed will quite certainly do more harm than good. Even quite young children talk about sex frankly, and many mothers have discovered with astonishment the extent of their children's knowledge, folklore and error. Your child is unlikely to remain 'pure', so he may as well be informed.

The most recent innovation in the primary school curriculum is the introduction of a foreign language, nearly always French. Children in independent preparatory schools have nearly always tackled not only French but Latin, though the teaching methods would normally make a primary school teacher's hair stand on end. Indeed, the feeling that older methods of language teaching were inimical to primary schools has put a lot of teachers off. But new approaches have shown that a foreign language can be assimilated into primary schools, and more of them are taking it up. In essence French is introduced in the same way that English was: children are introduced to words, phrases and then sentences in the new language. They become able to hold simple conversations. They are not inhibited by grammar: the fact that the verb 'to be' in French is quite as oddly conjugated as it is in English causes no more difficulty in the one language than it does in the other. Some schools manage to carry the practical application of language teaching even further and cart their children off for day trips to the French coast or even for a week or fortnight at a time.

The growth of French in primary schools has been greatly stimulated by the work of the Nuffield Foundation. You may find that your local primary school is engaged in what they call a Nuffield Project, not only in French but also in science and mathematics. The projects are large-scale attempts to prepare learning materials (notice they are no longer called teaching materials) with the cooperation of teachers, inspectors and the 'Schools Council' for the curriculum and examinations. If your child's school is engaged in one of them, you and he should be pleased, not only because the materials are themselves good but because their use is evidence of liveliness and a willingness to experiment.

There is one bizarre exception to the convention that what goes on in a school is a matter for the head teacher and his staff. Only one school subject, at the primary and secondary stage, has by law to be offered in all schools. This is not

English or mathematics or science but religious instruction. That this is so stems from educational history. The 1944 Education Act sought to offer secondary education for all. To do so, a very large number of Church schools had somehow to be brought within the normal system of education. Part of the bargain with the Churches which made this possible was the pair of sections in the Act which said that each school day must begin with a collective act of worship and that every school must offer religious instruction according to an agreed syllabus. Remember, though, that the compulsion rests upon the school. Children are not compelled to worship or to receive religious instruction: parents can withdraw them if they wish. Nor are teachers compelled to give religious instruction, though many believe that refusing to do so makes promotion less likely. It seems, from a number of less than satisfactory surveys, that most parents welcome some form of moral teaching in schools, even if they are hazy about its precise connection with particular religious beliefs. So for most parents there is probably little difficulty. On the other hand, you may be among the minority who regard religion as frivolous, or wicked, and then you do have a problem. What is more, religious instruction according to an agreed syllabus invariably means Christian instruction and it is thus objectionable to Jews, Hindus, Muslims and so on. All these groups of parents may well feel that they ought to withdraw their children and they can cheerfully do so if they are in large enough numbers. Often in these circumstances the school will provide religious teaching in a different faith, even though this may not be strictly legal. But what if your child is likely to be the only one withdrawn from religious instruction and worship? Here I suspect that it would be better to swallow your difficulties and let him join his classmates. The worship and the instruction these days are normally pretty vacuous in religious terms and the chances of corruption are slight. The burden of isolation, however light, is an unnecessary one.

With these the other school topics, what kind of support should parents give their children? Few expect to give them direct instruction in science, French or history. They quickly find that the tattered remnants of their own education can scarcely be made to cover any of their child's questions. Since there is so much less rote learning in school they cannot even offer to listen to memorized recitals. But this does not mean that they can or should do nothing. Children carry their school interests home with them and these can be encouraged or squashed by the reaction they evoke. I have already suggested that in mathematics parents might do worse than reverse the natural relationship. Instead of expecting to tell children things, and feeling embarrassed when they cannot, parents can ask. Primary school children are quite ready to tell their mothers where sugar and bread come from and happy to tell their fathers about plants growing in the garden or about public transport or the origin of the wood he is using to build a cupboard. Never ask, 'What did you do at school today?' It is a silly question and always gets a silly answer. It is far better to ask the children for information: you may be astonished at the expertise revealed. If you are sitting down to lunch, or taking a group of children on a jaunt and something comes to mind, try saying something like, 'Do any of you lot know . . . ?' Similarly, if you are asked a question which has you flummoxed, try to embark on finding out. And if you haven't a clue here either, ask the children. If you begin, 'Now, I wonder where we can find out about . . .', you may well find that the children will be off looking for the answer. The fact is that they are used to doing it, and may even offer the accolade of regarding you as a slightly dim version of their teacher.

Faced with the curiosity of young children parents are often enticed by an encyclopedia. Many of these are extremely expensive (well over £100 for multi-volume works) and some are still sold by disreputable door-to-door salesmanship. It is a good rule never to buy anything at your front door:

it deprives you of the simple opportunity of comparing what is available elsewhere. Even so, many families swear by their giant encyclopedia and constantly use it. A good single-volume one can be a great boon, as is a good dictionary. But there are now so very many good and cheap hand-books that you might like to consider a bundle of these as an alternative. The advantage is that each individual hand-book will be very much more informative than the relevant passage in an encyclopedia, and you can buy up books individually to meet the changing interests of the children. On the other hand, children do seem to like browsing through an encyclopedia and to enjoy absorbing the heaps of unrelated facts they find in it.

The same attitude of readiness to find out and competition in doing so can be extended to the normal business of daily life. A television programme may touch off a memory of some school project, or a new idea. More parents than ever are mobile, and children often get taken on journeys, frequently by car. This offers a good deal of opportunity which is often neglected. On Monday mornings children are sometimes asked to write up a sort of diary of what they did at the week-end. Some write, 'We went to the seaside'. If the teacher asks where they went, the children may reply, puzzled, 'to the seaside'. It does not occur to their parents to tell them where they are going, how far it is, what sort of country they are passing through, how much petrol the car consumes and so on. But there is no reason why children should not bring to their family journeys the same enquiring spirit as they bring to school work.

After all, families often find outings rather trying. Both parents and children may find that what was meant to be a treat has become a bore. Both can get more out of it if the enterprise is an exploration, if they find out about the place before they go, keep their wits about them while they are there and discuss and compare on the way home. None of this need be made formal. There is certainly no need to make sure that he has learned it. The new experience and the spirit of enquiry are as important as hoarded facts.

Ideally, a parent's relationship with teachers will enable him to get advice about an encyclopedia, family outings and home projects (particularly in the holidays) in the course of a normal chat. Teachers are usually ready to advise, particularly about books, if asked. Even if you don't get this sort of advice, you can still help the children best by applying the insight and methods of the primary school in natural and informal ways. This is a great bonus from educational methods and practices firmly based on the development and needs of the children. There need be no conflict between educational objectives at home and school. The one can reinforce the other. Above all, the process can be fun – for both children and their parents.

Indeed, 'playacting is all they ever seem to do', as one mother said of her son's infant school. It is scarcely an accurate or full description of the school's work, yet it does underline the concern of today's schools with the creative and imaginative lives of children. Basic skills, like writing, are essential: it is also important that children should have something worthwhile to write. This is why much of the school day is given to enlarging their experience by stretching the emotions and imaginations. Children learn by doing and by making: so drama, poetry, art and craft, music and movement take their place alongside reading and mathematics in their development and education. Not that any of these are distinctly separate 'subjects'. Drama and painting may grow naturally from history; craft work may arise in a geography project; poetry and music, or drama and movement, overlap and intermingle. The basic skills of reading and writing merge easily into creative English work.

Perhaps the amount and quality of children's writing is the most startling change in both primary and secondary schools. 'Creative writing' is a rather pompous name for it. It arises from children's own experience, personal or shared, from sights, sounds and smells, from a class visit or a weekend trip. Some parents are anxious about the revelations of home life that may come out in this way. (The essay on 'My Mother' which includes, 'She says sometimes, she wishes she was dead.') They should reflect that the best children's writing springs from the most deeply felt experience, and parents should be able to survive the remote possibility of embarrassment. Other parents fear that all this creation has meant a decline in neatness, good handwriting and accuracy. There is no evidence for this.

Children may be encouraged at school to write poems as well as prose, though most schools still approach poetry rather gingerly. Few teachers regularly speak poems to children, and some of the verse in school poetry books is rather dire. In some ways parents are better placed here than teachers. They can move naturally from reading stories and reciting nursery rhymes to reading poems they enjoy. Those parents who remember poems they themselves learned long ago are often surprised by their children's concentration as they declaim. Even children under five can often remember quite long poems if they hear them frequently, and they will be pleased later if they have not lost the habit of learning poetry by heart. Poetry written for adults is often better than children's verse (the pleasure of sound carries children over difficulties of language) but the best children's verse appeals also to adults. It is important that parents should enjoy it too.

Not all emotional and imaginative expression is verbal. In the infant school, even drama is more a matter of movement, gesture and mime than of speech. Young children may not have the vocabulary to improvise. Their lack of vocabulary can seriously limit their dramatic range. As they get older words force themselves in, and children are ready to perform simple plays written by others. Mummers' and mystery plays are often best because they echo in some of their conventions the children's own efforts.

At home there may be nothing so formal as the class play.

But children do not stop acting. They try on roles, as it were for size. They act out pleasurable experiences, so as to be cheered up again, and unpleasant ones, so as to come to terms with them. It is a great help if they have a box or a drawer full of old clothes and pieces of material for dressing up in. And if a child, being a doctor, advances on Mother as she is vacuuming the stairs, it would be nice if she could pause for a moment to be examined with stethoscope and spatula and then prescribed for with injections or pills. Parents need not feel they have to organize this sort of play. Often they are better out of the way, but they may come in quite handy as dummies or lay figures.

Drama, in today's schools, often shades into physical education. Parents may remember PT (physical training) with its tables of exercises designed for individual parts of the body (head, trunk, arms and legs), and they may remember drama only in connection with a failure to touch the toes or vault the horse. Today, most schools have a good deal of apparatus (climbing frames, ladders, bars and ropes) and children may refer not to PT or PE but to 'apparatus' as the name for what they do. Formal class teaching has given way to greater freedom, to movements of the whole body emphasizing activity, agility and skill. In addition, physical education has been influenced by the principles of dance-drama. Children may be asked to be as big, wide or tall as they can be, to walk, or run as heavily or lightly as they can, to be a horse or a lion or a snake, to express anger, fear, happiness or pride. In all this they will be using their bodies to the full – and their minds and emotions as well.

Not that this exhausts physical education. As children grow older they will be introduced to the various team games like netball, football and cricket. If they are lucky they will learn to swim.

Very few homes can provide the range of possibilities a school offers for physical education. This is one reason, after all, for sending children to school. (Even the most unplanned family is unlikely to field two football sides.) This is all the more reason for visits to local parks and day trips into the country or the seaside at weekends and in the school holidays. If you have a garden, let the children have some of it. They will make a mess and damage things (though they can learn to respect other people's property) but the garden can be reclaimed when they grow up and you can potter peacefully in retirement.

Swimming is especially attractive: it is fun, it is good exercise and it might save a child's life. Many schools take children to the local baths (some have their own baths, often built by the parents) but whether they do or not, parents can.

Some parents buy dancing classes for their children, especially though not only for girls. Some may have visions of the ballet. Normally parents should let their children go to formal lessons if the children themselves want to. If the interest wanes, let them stop. There is no sense in urging, bribing or forcing a primary school child into some sort of career choice. At school, movement will be accompanied by music either on the piano or gramophone. Children will also make their own music, in singing or with instruments. Probably parents will remember the percussion band of their own schools days and elementary musical reading ('ta-tay-ta-tay-tah tah'). These still exist, though many schools have added recorders to the repertoire. Others, especially those with freer methods, have xylophones and tubular bells available in the classroom for children to experiment on. Some junior schools have visiting teachers for the piano, violin, or more rarely, wind instruments.

Learning a musical instrument has been a fairly common fate for many children. It has frequently caused misery. Parents will not go far wrong if they remember that the object of the exercise is to give pleasure, to the children and to others. If parents are themselves musical, listening a lot or playing an instrument themselves, children will take an interest fairly naturally. If there is a piano in the house they will experiment: some will mess about, others will work off their aggression, but some will try out combinations and sequences of notes and show more than sporadic interest. Perhaps they would enjoy lessons: at any rate let them try. There will be the inevitable stretches of backsliding and boredom. Tact is needed here, and perhaps parents are not best placed to exercise it (they are paying the bill and thus abhor waste). Children benefit from the discipline of consistent effort, and their music teacher should be able to get it from them. If parents find themselves constantly nagging a child to practise they should think of calling it off and buying a new carpet for the dining room instead.

At one time musical teaching, even for the young, was highly theoretical, then a reaction set in and theory almost disappeared. Some children enjoy the theory: it is the same pleasure as that of discovering how something works. And some children are able to compose short tunes. Let them. But as with dancing, don't dream of the future. The child may be a Wokingham Mozart, but the point of music when he is young is that it should be fun.

So should all kinds of art and craft. All children enjoy drawing, painting, cutting up, modelling, and so on. They do a lot of this at school, and most schools have been convinced by the movement towards freedom in art. So children's paintings are vivid, colourful, bold, original and often show a good grasp of how to organize the flat surface of the paper. When children bring their efforts home, a parent's instinct is to display them somewhere. Quite right too. And if children have a room of their own a board for pinning things on is a boon. Let them make their own Christmas cards and birthday cards for friends and relatives. These are more fun to receive than printed ones and are much cheaper. Letting children do 'thank you' cards or pictures is more rewarding than 'thank you' letters, for both sides. Cut-out and stand-up models are now common in comics and cereal packets: but once they know the principle children can draw and cut out their own models. One difficulty for parents is to adjust to the pace at which children work. They may take half a term to make a book at school: so don't expect them to complete an idea at home in an afternoon.

At school children may meet basket-making, book-binding, weaving, block-printing, clay modelling, even pottery. At home they can enjoy the more traditional knitting, sewing and woodwork, though there is no need to confine these traditionally to either girls or boys.

And children cannot and should not rely entirely on their own inner resources any more than adults do. The television can stimulate the imagination and the mind. Children can enjoy films, the theatre, pantomimes, concerts, even cathedral architecture and art exhibitions. Take them if you can, but remember that the purpose is delight. If it becomes a bore go out for an ice cream.

7 Transfer to Secondary Schools

The point of transfer from primary to secondary schools at the age of eleven has become something of an event in children's lives. But it is one that dates back only to 1944. Before the great Education Act of that year most children simply stayed in their elementary schools until the school-leaving age, but in 1944 education was organized in 'three progressive stages': primary, secondary and further. Movement from one to the other was meant to involve a change of educational experience. As we shall see in this and the next chapter, secondary schools are normally larger and more formally organized than primary schools. They are designed less for children and more for adolescents. They have the laboratories, work shops, craft rooms and gymnasia to accommodate and meet the growing physical skills of their pupils. They emphasize systematic learning, precision and specialization, of which pupils become capable and which, up to a point, they demand as they get older. Formal class teaching becomes normal and the demands of the syllabus assume recognized importance.

Clearly the age at which children transfer to this new educational atmosphere should depend on the point at which they are ready for it. But, as the first chapter of this book showed, children differ widely in their rates of development. Girls reach puberty, on average, two years earlier than boys, and there may be four years' variation between *normal* boys or girls. In fact the age of eleven became the age of transfer in 1944 less for educational and developmental reasons than for practical ones. With a school-leaving age of 15 it was the age which would give most children a reasonable length of secondary school course.

Of course, there is an added reason why the point of transfer has loomed so large for children and their parents. Since 1944 secondary education has been offered in different types of schools. Most areas have grammar and secondary modern schools; a few have technical schools as well; and some have experiments, anomalies or relics from bygone ages. You will look in vain for anything about all this in the 1944 Education Act. Although the act promises 'secondary education for all', it was simply assumed at the time that this could not possibly mean that all children would be offered a similar education after eleven. In a sense this was simply making the best of what there was. The 1944 Act may have produced a new legal framework for education; the schools and the teachers remained and had to be used. Nor was there very much sense that this was a bad thing. The theory and practice of education had been thoroughly studied by official committees before the war, and legislators assumed that the task was simply to create the means by which these pre-war ideas came at last to be put into effect.

What happened, at all events, was that the schools which before 1944 had been called 'secondary' became grammar schools and that many pre-war elementary or all-age schools lost their junior pupils and became secondary modern schools. Officially it was said that the distinguishing feature of a grammar school course lay in 'its length, in the scholarly treatment of its content and in the stern intellectual discipline' it afforded. Its concentration on courses leading to ordinary and advanced levels of the General Certificate of Education and its breadth of curriculum recall the pre-war regulation which said that a secondary school was one for pupils who intended to remain there at least until they were sixteen; which offered a general education including mathematics, science and languages – and which was, in addition, a recognized preliminary to courses of further and higher education.

Officially, too, it was expected that the secondary modern schools would offer 'a good all round secondary education not focusing primarily on the traditional subjects of the school curriculum but developing out of the interests of the children'. In other words, there was no determination that the secondary modern schools should be secondary in the pre-war sense, though it was hoped that teachers in them would experiment and themselves discover what kind of education their pupils should be offered. With some notable exceptions, secondary modern schools tended to offer a curriculum which simply lacked such components as science, mathematics and languages; such an education is secondary only in name.

But if a local authority has different kinds of secondary schools there has to be some method of deciding which children should go to which. So all children have undergone a selection process at about the age of ten, which, with British logic, has become generally known as the eleven plus. The methods of selection have been fairly standard among local authorities, because there has been a genuine attempt to see that they are objective and without bias. At the heart of them are tests which have sought to measure a child's innate ability, free from the handicaps or advantages of a particular background or teaching. These tests have been variously known as intelligence or verbal reasoning tests. In addition, authorities have used the more familiar tests of attainment in, for example, English or arithmetic (these could be simply a matter of doing a given number of sums of a certain level within a given time), and some authorities also set an English essay.

At first these tests were commonly given in a batch on the same day, but increasingly they have been spread over a longer period and extra information has been taken into account. This might include a child's record throughout the last year or couple of years in his primary school, teachers' assessments of his capabilities or even, in some cases, an interview with the child and (more rarely) his parents.

When the tests are completed and marked the children in the area are listed in order of ability, as measured, and the grammar school places available are offered to those at the top of the list. If there are any technical schools, places in them are offered either as an alternative to the children at the top of the list or to those a little lower down. The rest of the children are offered places in secondary modern schools. As we shall see, there is a lot to be said against both the process and the philosophy behind it, but we should admit at least that the eleven plus procedures have been probably as fair and accurate as such procedures can ever be.

An attempt was also made to reduce discrepancies between the various kinds of schools. All secondary schools were to have 'parity of esteem' and of accommodation and equipment. In buildings and cost of equipment, at any rate, this parity was achieved, but because the grammar schools accommodated children beyond school-leaving age and offered an academic education, they tended to be staffed and equipped differently. They had, for example, three times as many graduates as secondary modern schools and were given laboratories rather than craft rooms. The educational opportunities offered in the two types of schools continued to be markedly different.

The selection of children for various kinds of school was not simply a matter of expediency. As we have seen, there was an official justification for different kinds of secondary education, and, for a time, an overwhelming majority of educational opinion favoured it. The defence of selection rested upon three basic assumptions. The first is that levels of ability stay roughly constant, at least from the age of eleven onwards, and that they can be accurately measured. The second is that only a recognizable minority of children are able to benefit from an academic, grammar school (or, as I would say, secondary) education. The third is that children's abilities differ and require different kinds of schools: in particular it was and is asserted that the brighter children would be held back if they were educated with the rest. As the years have gone by it has become clear that all these assumptions are false and that there is no educational justification for selecting different children for different kinds of schools at eleven.

Because there is still a lot of argument about it, let us look at these assumptions a little more closely, beginning with the one about levels of ability. In the most objective of the eleven plus tests, those of intelligence, the results give each child an 'intelligence quotient' or I.Q. To put it crudely, this is a way of describing how the child's mental age compares with his physical age. A child who achieves in a test what the average ten-year-old achieves can be said to have a mental age of ten, and this is expressed as an I.Q. by dividing his mental age by his physical age and multiplying the result by 100. Our ten-year-old who performs like an average ten-year-old has an I.Q. of $\frac{10}{10}$ x 100, which equals 100. Thus an average I.Q. is 100. If, on the other hand, a child of ten has a mental age of twelve, his I.Q. is $\frac{12}{10}$ x 100 which is 120. The better a child performs in an intelligence test, the further above 100 his I.Q. will be. The child who performs less well will have an I.Q. of less than 100.

Putting it in a mathematical form like this makes intelligence look as if it can be measured very precisely. If it were so, it would presumably be reasonable to use I.Qs. to determine what sort of school children should go to. The trouble is that the measurement is nowhere near as precise as it looks, for a number of reasons. In the first place, performance can vary greatly from one test to another, so a single test may produce an I.Q. which is simply wrong. Over a period of years the difference may be much greater, so that a decision based upon a test taken at eleven may turn out to be mistaken a year or two later. If a child has an I.Q. of 95, the best that we can say is that there is a ten to one chance that over the years it will be between 80 and 110. Precision has eluded us. This is catastrophic for the selection process, which depends upon distinguishing between children of very similar I.Qs. Drawing a line between those with I.Qs. of 126 and those of 125 (however this may be modified by scores in other tests or by teachers' record cards), and sending some to grammar schools and others to secondary modern schools, is absurd and unjust.

Nor are even I.Q. tests as objective as was at first thought. They do something to allow for differences of educational background and experience; but nowhere near enough. The tests, although ostensibly educational, are in effect social. The children of manual workers and poorly educated parents are likely to do less well in normal intelligence tests. The mechanics by which this discrepancy occurs are still not thoroughly understood. But the hope that we can offer genuine equality of opportunity to all children through selection by 'ability' has turned out to be false. Of course, there are a whole lot of qualities quite as necessary for success in school and in later life that cannot be measured at present even as crudely as we measure intelligence: qualities like conscientiousness, judgement, creativeness and industry, for example.

But even if precise measurement of abilities were possible, to be happy about separating children into quite different kinds of schools we should have to be sure that their abilities did not change very much as they grew older. But this goes against everything that we know about children's growth and development, which has been outlined in Chapter 1. We saw there that, to take a simple point, children develop at different rates, so an examination bound to the age of ten or eleven is likely to penalize some of them. A more important point is that, since a child's characteristics are a result not of heredity alone, nor of environment alone, but of the interaction between the two, what you do to a child makes a difference to him. You can improve or impair his abilities. Education actually works. School is not just a place where children learn useful knowledge: it is a place where they develop their abilities. If a child's capacity is fixed at eleven, half the point of going to secondary school at all is lost. This view of intelligence has come to be accepted gradually over a long period, but it was first officially endorsed in 1963 when the Newsom Report was published and the then Minister of Education, Sir Edward Boyle, wrote in its foreword: 'the essential point is that all children should have equal opportunity of *acquiring intelligence* ...' (my italics). If you think of schools as places where children acquire intelligence you become less confident of using the measurement of intelligence to sort them out into different schools. And it is not the job of teachers to accept a test score as in any way final. Indeed, it is not too much to say that a teacher's job is to try to falsify tests, to help the child achieve things of which he seemed incapable.

The second assumption behind selection – that there is a small minority of academic children – is equally dubious. In the first place there have now been a whole lot of government and other reports containing surveys which showed that there were as many able children outside grammar schools as inside them; large numbers of 'suitable' children were not being selected. In the second place, modification or even abolition of selection has shown in practice that very many more than the previously accepted minority can take an academic education. This, of course, is what one might expect from the fact that the proportion of children going to grammar school varies from one part of the country to another. In some places three out of every seven do so. In others the proportion is only one in seven. It is, to say the least, unlikely that the minority capable of benefiting from grammar schools reflects such dramatic differences in local abilities. Nor has it turned out to be sensible to offer to less academic children a more limited curriculum. The effect in too many cases was a simply stultifying curriculum in the secondary modern schools. This, according to one view, could actually reduce the intelligence of the pupils over the course of their school life.

This leads to the last assumption behind selection: that separate schools are needed for separate abilities. Of course, children differ and have different needs. This is not in question; what is in doubt is how these needs are to be met, and it is at best an act of faith to assert that the very wide diversity of children can somehow be met by two or three kinds of secondary school. What we need is the greatest variety of provision and the argument is about how to secure it. The form in which this particular assumption has been expressed casts its own doubt upon it. One of the staunchest defenders of selection has said recently that it had been a great error to concentrate on defending grammar schools and to neglect the campaign to save the secondary moderns. Maybe there were very few people indeed who could ever be found to claim that secondary modern schools were on the whole the best way of meeting the educational needs of the children in them. Of course teachers in them defended what they were doing: one cannot do a job like teaching for any length of time without having some kind of intellectual and emotional justification for it. But in fact there has never been a confident and persuasive justification for this type of school. Commentators from outside have been much less charitable. One American educator, for example, described them as custodial rather than educational institutions. He was not sneering at the pupils or the teachers, except in so far as the latter were unconscious or complacent about what they were doing. What he was saying was that they had been given an impossible job.

The chief defence of different schools has in fact come from those who are concerned with the needs and interests of the academic minority in grammar schools. The terms in which they couch the arguments are often national. The country, they say, depends upon the brains of its most able and these are a scarce resource which must be husbanded. The implication is that these brains will in the end be less effective if their possessors are educated in the same schools as most children.

But will the bright child be held back if he is not separated from the other children? Many of the fears about this come from what people think happens in American high schools which have always been non-selective. A straight comparison is hard to make because the faults and virtues of American schools come from traditions and practices of education which are different from our own; but it might be said in passing that the proportion of children and young people attaining high achievement at various levels in the two countries does little to support the idea of a lack of opportunity for intelligence in America. Far more of the bright children in America are sent by their schools into higher education than in Britain. Nor does experience here suggest that more able people suffer in non-selective schools. When former grammar schools have been extended into comprehensive schools they normally found that more, rather than fewer, of their academic pupils stay longer, pass examinations and go to university. There is deplorably little evidence about all this in Britain. None of those worthy, heavy official reports on education since the war has specifically considered selection for different kinds of secondary education. But simple experience shows that it is not necessary.

It is not only that the assumptions behind selection are wrong: the consequences in practice are also unhappy. The tests at eleven plus distort the curriculum of the primary schools, however much they were designed to avoid this. Teachers feel uneasy about introducing new methods or subjects when they know that their pupils will in the event be sitting an external leaving examination, and 'preparation' for the eleven plus (which the teachers concerned unconvincingly distinguish from coaching) very often dominates the last years of primary education. In some schools one might be forgiven for thinking that it was the major purpose of education. The eleven plus procedures also contribute to the continuation of 'streaming' by ability. Whatever the merits of the argument, streaming is thought to be inevitable while the eleven plus lasts, although a growing number of primary school teachers are anxious for its end.

In secondary education the difficulties facing the secondary moderns are enormous and in most of them overwhelming. Whatever the official explanation, or the claims of the teachers, parents and pupils continue to feel that these are schools for failures. A sense of rejection and demoralization is general and has been surmounted by only exceptional schools. The idea that the children who do not fit into the grammar schools are those in some way 'good with their hands' is patronizing, sentimental and inaccurate.

There have been, of course, a number of secondary moderns which managed in spite of everything to encourage academic work and to offer their pupils growing opportunities. They enter pupils for the General Certificate of Education at O level and for the Certificate of Secondary Education, but paradoxically these schools call into question the whole selective process. The more children who are shown to be academically capable, after rejection at eleven, on the same terms as those who have been selected at that age, the less rational it seems to select at all. It may be that these children have been enabled to do well precisely because they have not entered the more demanding atmosphere of the grammar schools (a point which has been argued by defenders of selection), but this looks more like an argument for enabling schools to treat all pupils according to their needs rather than one for rigid divisions into kinds of schools.

The finality of the process is indeed almost complete, although many authorities insist that it is possible for pupils to move later from secondary modern schools to grammar schools if they show themselves capable of benefiting from the change. Unfortunately, as common sense would suggest, the longer a pupil stays in one school with one set of attitudes and syllabuses, the less likely he is to show himself capable of meeting the demands of another. Since the grammar schools have been the recognized route to higher education and the professions, and particularly to universities, it is a child's future which is being decided at the age of eleven. Indeed, one international study of university admissions concluded that the admission process to British universities began at the end of primary education when three-quarters of the children were effectively prevented from embarking on preparation for it.

It is fair to say that at first the eleven plus process was regarded as an educational and social breakthrough offering opportunity where this did not exist before. Until the 1944 Education Act, opportunity existed for the relatively rich: after that date it was made available to the relatively clever. One of the most persistent defences of the post-war system has been that it has enabled clever children of poor or uneducated parents to make the most of themselves. As a result of a number of studies we have had to modify our enthusiasm about the extent to which this opportunity is actually available. Our arrangements still seem to favour the relatively rich. But, if we are now seeking to change selection at eleven, we must remember that it served the purpose of widening opportunities a quarter of a century ago and that our object now is not to go back on the ideals of 1944, but to extend them and to make opportunity yet more widely available.

Dissatisfaction with selection at eleven grew generally among professional educators: among teachers, psychologists, sociologists and others. But in education change occurs very slowly as a rule. What has hastened the end of the eleven plus is that dissatisfaction with it has become general among parents. They instinctively realize what it has taken a good deal of research to establish formally. Parents may not be able to say clearly why the educational assumptions behind it are wrong, but they do know how selection affects their own children and they do not like what they know. The eleven plus is almost universally unpopular amongst those who have had experience of it. The dislike was expressed in common sense terms because it was founded in common sense.

First of all parents saw very clearly the differences in educational opportunity offered in different kinds of school, and many of them resented these differences. The official attempt to convince them that all schools had 'parity of esteem' came quickly to be regarded as a cynical piece of administrators' double talk. Similarly, even parents who had never heard of the idea of the developmental age knew from simple observation that children develop at different rates. They knew that a child's performance might vary from day to day, and without knowing even the name sociology they sensed that different home backgrounds of children might greatly affect their performance in schools and in examinations. So they knew that a test or series of tests taken at one age would favour children who develop earlier and penalize those who develop later. They might have guessed, even if they did not know the evidence, that such tests penalize the younger children of an age group as well as those of poorer parents. The injustice of making a child's future depend upon his performance in a single day's tests was so obvious that local authorities soon came to spread the tests over a longer period, but parental anger and frustration were not very much diminished.

At first this anger was directed against the tests themselves – to which there was the obvious answer that these were the best that could be devised. Even so, local authorities became very sensitive about them. The research bodies which designed the tests were prevented from saying publicly which authorities used which kinds. The tests themselves were kept secret, particularly with a view to discouraging coaching, but the consequence of this was that parents became even more worried than they need have been and that commercial versions of specimen tests were a sell-out. But gradually the parents came to realize that it was not the tests themselves which were objectionable, but the whole process of selection.

In a book about the relations between home and school it

is as well to emphasize the importance of this. I do not believe that any amount of effort by teachers and other professional people could have altered so firmly established a practice as selection, with all its physical expression in different school buildings, unless the effort had chimed with the public mood. The most obvious expression of this lay in the democratic process. From the middle or late 1950s the Labour and Liberal parties were committed to end selection. By the mid-1960s the Conservative party had realized that it would be electorally disastrous to be labelled as defenders of the eleven plus. The education service itself has said surprisingly little formally on the subject. None of the three major Central Advisory Council reports considered it directly, and there has been no departmental committee either on selection or on the practicalities of comprehensive schools. In my view, the ending of selection is a reform which is being carried through because most people want it, and parents can feel that the education service is responsive to their wishes at least to this extent. In spite of difficulties and setbacks, the ending of selection is as near a national policy as anything in education could be.

But ending selection is only half the argument. The next question is, what do we put in its place? As with most public policies parents may be quite able to say what it is that they dislike about the present state of affairs; it is not reasonable to expect them to know precisely what would improve matters. This is the job of politicians and professionals. In a sense, though, the answer is obvious. If you decide not to select for different kinds of schools at the beginning of the secondary stage, then the obvious thing is for children simply to go to their local secondary school, as they go at five to their local primary school. You then have to see that all secondary schools are able to accommodate children of all levels of ability and offer them a full secondary range of courses. Such schools have come to be called 'comprehensive' schools, though the thing to remember is that primary schools have always been comprehensive schools: there is nothing mysterious in the term.

The positive arguments for comprehensive schools are: first, that opportunities remain open for all children, up to the school-leaving age. No hard-and-fast tests need to be made at eleven or thirteen or even later. The second advantage is that such schools can offer a tremendous variety of courses. This is partly because they are large schools, which means that they can employ teachers for particular interests or in unpopular subjects without weakening the basic provision they make for the more normal curriculum. Indeed, the teachers can be much more flexibly employed in other ways too. In a selective system the graduates are concentrated in the grammar schools. This means that the non-graduate teachers may not get very much chance of teaching the children of highest measured ability. It may also mean that most children rarely get taught by graduates. Of course, many of the opponents of comprehensive schools say that in these schools the graduates are spread too thin, so that nobody benefits from the academic and specialist contributions they might otherwise make. Up to a point this is a variation of the concern for the most able children; but it relates to the number of graduates available.

There really is likely to be a shortage, particularly of science and mathematics teachers, in the future and it is a genuine question, how scarce teachers can best be used; and the question remains even if we do not make the basic mistake of assuming that the graduate is necessarily a better teacher. What the defenders of comprehensive schools would argue is that decisions about deployment of staff are best made by head teachers in consultation with their colleagues, and not as a by-product of an administrative arrangement like selection for different kinds of schools. A head may possibly think his graduates should concentrate on the academic children, with a quarter of their time spent on the others. But in a selective system a decision of this sort is not possible, because the distribution of graduates is determined outside the individual school.

A final positive argument for comprehensive schools is that their introduction would mean that all children would share a common educational experience, at least up to the school-leaving age. The hope is that children of all levels of ability and social background will learn to live and mix together. It has to be admitted that in practice comprehensive schools may remain a long way from realizing this aspiration. In the first place, if all the children from the neighbourhood go to the local school, the school may in effect be composed of pupils from a fairly narrow social class. Opponents of comprehensives make much of this and claim that a grammar school may really be much more socially mixed than this. The answer is that comprehensive schools are no worse in this respect than the secondary moderns to which most children in any case go; indeed, they are that much better since they contain a fuller range of ability. At the same time, as we have seen, the grammar schools certainly do not reflect the social mixture of the country as a whole: they are heavily over-populated by middle-class children. In short, both the more extravagant claims for social mixing in comprehensive schools and the more romantic views of the grammar school contribution to this end are equally mistaken.

More seriously, for many of the staunchest defenders of comprehensive schools, these schools normally continue to 'stream' by ability and thus reproduce within the school the very divisions which their existence seeks to eliminate. It may be almost as easy for the children who would have gone to a grammar school to remain aloof from the rest as if they had actually done so. The answer here is that in a selective system this is inevitable; in a comprehensive school it is possible to avoid or mitigate it. What is more, the decision to end streaming by ability can be taken by the head and staff of a school and carried through by them. As we shall see, a decision to abolish selection involves considerable political and administrative upheaval. 'Going comprehensive' does not ensure that class teachers change their practices. Neither does it guarantee that they improve. All the country can do with a change of this kind is to make it possible for the schools to do a better job. British teachers are proud of their independence: it is they who will make comprehensive schools succeed or fail.

Naturally, comprehensive schools have not suddenly burst upon the educational scene. It often surprises people to discover how much experience there has been of them in various parts of the country. The reason why this experience has been possible is that schools in Great Britain, as we shall see in Chapter 12, are the responsibility of local education authorities. Since 1974 these have been the councils of the new counties and metropolitan districts, the outer London boroughs and a committee of the Greater London Council called the Inner London Education Authority. (Before that, county boroughs were education authorities, but they no longer exist.) It is they who must see that there are enough schools in their areas and they who decide on the pattern of secondary education. The local authorities are not completely free: the government controls, for example, the amount and standards of educational buildings. Since the war a number of authorities have built comprehensive schools. Usually these schools have been built within a new housing development or in rural areas. In both circumstances it seemed odd to establish a selective system from scratch. On the other hand, it is probably true to say that the larger city authorities, like London, Coventry and Bristol, established their comprehensives at least partly because they believed in the change for educational and social reasons; whereas county authorities like Anglesey and Devon did so for the practical reason that they would otherwise have had to establish very small unsatisfactory rural grammar schools. In other authorities there had been a debate about the establishment of comprehensive schools and many different ideas had emerged as a result of this; when a national policy for reorganizing secondary education on comprehensive lines was accepted by Parliament, there was already a great deal of experience on how it might be done.

The change came in 1965 when a resolution of the House of Commons said: 'That this House, conscious of the need to raise educational standards at all levels, and regretting that the realization of this objective is impeded by the separation of children into different types of secondary schools, notes with approval the efforts of local authorities to reorganize secondary education on comprehensive lines which will preserve all that is valuable in grammar school education for those children who now receive it and make it available to more children; recognizes that the method and timing of such reorganization should vary to meet local needs; and believes that the time is now ripe for a declaration of national policy.'

In July of the same year the Department of Education and Science sent out a circular to local authorities, Circular 10/65, saying that the Secretary of State 'requests local education authorities, if they have not already done so, to prepare and submit to him plans for reorganizing secondary education in their areas on comprehensive lines' and giving some guidance on how to do it.

You will notice that the Secretary of State merely 'requested': he had no power to compel local authorities. The hope at the time, which has largely been realized, was that there was sufficient momentum for reorganization and that most local authorities would wish to do so voluntarily. There were in fact a handful of authorities, of which the most significant was Birmingham, which either refused outright or dragged their feet.

Nor did the circular lay down how local authorities should effect reorganization. What the circular did was to offer guidance. The organization and administration of schools was and is recognized to be a local matter. This is one reason why you will find that details of comprehensive reorganization vary substantially from one part of the country to another.

Circular 10/65 in fact suggested six ways of 'going comprehensive'. Most of them had already been tried somewhere or other. What the circular said was that, although the needs of children were much the same everywhere, the precise way in which each authority decided to reorganize would depend upon its own views, the distribution of population and the schools already existing. It was important, the circular added, 'that new schemes should build on the foundations of present achievements and preserve what is best in individual schools'.

The six ways of 'going comprehensive' were as follows, although the order in which they appeared in the circular was rather different:

(a) A school taking all the secondary school children in a neighbourhood, aged from eleven to eighteen, and offering them a full range of courses. This the circular called the 'orthodox comprehensive school' and said that it would provide the simplest and best solution if the country was starting a new pattern of secondary education from scratch. It added that a six- or seven-form entry would be a reasonable size for a school of this type. Such a school might have about 1,000 children in it altogether, but the circular very much discouraged the authorities from adopting this solution where the buildings were not big enough and where the pupils would have to be distributed between a number of buildings. Authorities which have put up such schemes have been urged by the Department to think again.

An advantage of the all-through school is that pupils' educational experience can most easily be planned as a whole. An advantage, on balance, too, is the large size. In short, size brings variety and choice. A small school may be able to offer only one foreign language: a large one half a dozen. The range of accommodation and equipment can be very much greater. There is a tradition of cosiness in British education, in which a headmaster knows every boy by his name, but this seldom compensates for the limitations of small schools, and in any case large ones are evolving careful methods like the use of tutorial systems to ensure that pupils are not neglected.

(b) A system in which all the pupils go from their primary school to a comprehensive school at eleven and then transfer from this to another comprehensive school at thirteen or fourteen is known as a 'two-tier' system. These two-tier arrangements would be very much less popular if they did not offer a way of using existing buildings. They do involve a second change of school after only two or three years and this can make an unwelcome break in the pupil's educational experience unless there is very close collaboration between the two tiers. On the other hand, there are positive advantages: many people claim that the full eleven to eighteen age range is too wide to be successfully accommodated in one school; so that separating the younger from the older pupils makes it easier to create institutions more appropriate for each.

(c) After the Education Act of 1964 local authorities became able to vary the age of transfer from primary to secondary school; and this has enabled some of them to create comprehensive schemes including 'middle' schools. Under this system pupils are in primary schools until the age of eight or nine, in middle schools until thirteen or fourteen and in upper schools from then onwards; and all these schools are comprehensive. Here again, authorities may go for a middle-school solution because it enables them to make the best use of existing buildings: former grammar schools can be used as senior schools and former secondary modern schools as middle schools. But the arrangement has very positive educational justifications. For example, the Plowden Report on primary education recommended that the age of transfer to secondary schools should be raised to twelve and felt that thirteen would almost be equally appropriate. It pointed out that primary education would then be divided into 'lower' and 'middle' schools.

This means that methods which have shown so much success at the primary stage can be continued into what is now the secondary stage, and subjects like languages, which have hitherto been taught in only secondary schools, can be introduced to children at primary age. As with the two-tier system, schools with pupils entering at twelve or thirteen can be much more adult institutions.

(d) Schools in which pupils go to comprehensive schools from eleven to fifteen or sixteen while those who are staying on into the sixth form do so in a separate institution are known as sixth-form college schemes. In some places a sixth-form college serving a number of lower schools is attached to one of these schools. Again, a number of authorities have found it convenient to turn existing grammar schools into sixth-form colleges, and one or two of them are toying with the idea of linking the sixth-form college with a local technical college of further education. The advantage claimed for this arrangement is that the sixth-formers can be offered an institution specifically designed for them in which they can be treated more as young adults or students than as children or pupils. Its opponents claim that it is a bad thing to cut off the younger age groups from the influence of the sixth form and that the need to transfer to another school at the school-leaving age may discourage pupils from staying on.

All these four variations of comprehensive schools were mentioned by the circular as acceptable long-term methods of reorganizing the secondary schools on comprehensive lines, but it added a couple of 'interim' arrangements which might be acceptable in the short term, to help an authority over the difficult translation from a selective to a comprehensive system. Both involved variations on a scheme developed in the county of Leicestershire (thus known as the Leicestershire scheme), in which all pupils transferred to comprehensive schools at the age of eleven, but children whose parents promised to keep them at school until the age of sixteen were treated differently at the age of thirteen or fourteen from the rest. Sometimes they were transferred to 'grammar' schools, sometimes all the children moved, some to schools which accommodated them only up to the school-leaving age and other schools taking them on to eighteen. Though the defenders of these schemes claimed that they were based upon parental choice, the circular stated that they retained an element of selection and were unsuitable long-term solutions. Leicestershire has itself moved away from the Leicestershire scheme.

There is little doubt that the judgement implied in Circular 10/65, that local authorities were ready to reorganize secondary education, turned out to be right. In fact, nearly 100 local authorities had such plans, in varying stages of preparation and detail, even before the circular was issued. Most of them in fact submitted schemes. In this they were 'encouraged' by another circular in the following year which stated that the Secretary of State would not approve future building projects unless these were compatible with reorganization. In effect this meant that he would not approve new buildings for small schools or plans which were specifically designated 'grammar' or 'secondary modern'. As time went on even reluctant local authorities found that there was a good deal of local pressure for abolishing selection, and some were persuaded by campaigners organized for this purpose.

With a change of government, Circular 10/65 was withdrawn and replaced by Circular 10/70. This was very short and said authorities with approved plans could implement or modify them and those with plans awaiting decision could leave them to be considered or withdraw them. It particularly enjoined local authorities to discuss plans with teachers and to give parents the chance to make their views known before decisions were taken.

At first Circular 10/70 had almost no effect. Two local authorities withdrew plans for reorganization which had not yet been approved. Two others decided that since they were no longer compelled to abolish selection they might as well go ahead and abolish it. But gradually it became clear that the Secretary of State was treating each proposal for changing schools separately, rather than as part of a local authority's reorganization plan. This meant that an authority might see most of its proposals approved and some rejected. The rejections usually involved retaining grammar schools, and this might undermine the sense and purpose of the whole scheme. Equally important was the decision to concentrate all the money available for improving and replacing schools on the primary stage. This slowed down the change where local authorities were relying on building money to help them to reorganize.

With yet another change of Government in 1974, a new circular, 4/74, reaffirmed the determination to develop a fully comprehensive system of secondary education and to end 'selection at 11 plus or at any other stage'. Authorities were again asked to proceed with their own proposals.

The upshot of all these circulars and building programmes, however, is that secondary education is being reorganized all over the country but in many different ways and at many different rates. All the four ways of going comprehensive mentioned in Circular 10/65 are being used in some part of the country or other, and they are all in various stages of completion. In other words, secondary education will be in a state of change (some would say chaos) for many years to come, and people who move from one part of the country to another will find very different arrangements in practice. In some places selection will still be used, although it will gradually disappear. Elsewhere, parents may find unfamiliar kinds of comprehensive schools. Eventually, of course, all the schools will be comprehensive, and once you abolish selection at eleven it is less important that every local authority in the land has the same pattern of secondary education. A genuine variety is emerging which was not possible under the old arrangements, and one consequence of the change will be a greatly enlarged possibility of genuine parental choice. Perhaps one example of this will suffice. Most of the City of Bristol is served by comprehensive schools. Each school is bound to take all the children from its neighbourhood who apply to go to it, and each school is able to offer a full second-ary range of courses up to the highest levels. But each school is also developing a strong interest in a particular aspect of the curriculum: one is strong in languages; another has an arts centre; a third is developing new courses in sciences; a fourth is strong in mathematics. A Bristol child who wants to choose a particular school because he has a particular interest is increasingly able to do so, and indeed the authority provides transport for the children across the city. The point to remem-ber is that this kind of choice is not possible unless it can be made in the knowledge that every school is able to offer a comparable secondary education. It was not possible in a selective system, where choices between the kinds of educa-tion available were marred by the fact that they also involved differences in quality and extent of education.

Of the 104 authorities in England and Wales, 17 have completed their reorganization into a comprehensive system, and another eight have reorganized their county but not their voluntary schools. Seventy-eight authorities are partially re-organized, and only one has not reorganized at all. There are now 1,600 comprehensive schools in England and Wales ac-commodating 1,400,000 pupils, or 41 per cent of the secondary school population.

It remains only to describe what happens at the point of transfer. In the January of your child's last year at primary school, you will get an official notice from the chief education officer. This will say that your child will be transferred to a secondary school in the following September and will set out the arrangements the local authority has made. The letter will also enclose a form offering you a choice, if this is possible. (The law and practice of parental choice have already been fully described in Chapter 3.) If you have any questions, the person to consult is the teacher or head at the primary school. If you find yourself in any difficulty you may be involved in an interview with the education officer or his officials, with councillors or members of the education committee and so on, but the best starting place is your child's present teacher. Assuming the question of choice goes well, you are then likely to get another letter in the summer confirming the school to which your child is expected to go by the education officer and asking you to sign a form of acceptance. It is probably fair to say that objections are most likely to arise in those areas where selection takes place when children have been allocated to secondary moderns which parents in any case regard as unacceptably bad. But the spread of comprehensive education inevitably means that parents may be dissatisfied with particular comprehensive schools, and their doubts and fears may be increased by an over-rigid attitude on the part of the authority. Parents in this position might consult Chapter 3.

Whatever the system of secondary education or the particular school to which your child goes at eleven, the transfer to secondary school can be both stimulating and trying. For the children it resembles their first introduction to school – that initial point of transfer from home to school at five. It offers similar challenges and problems. All children are stimulated by novelty and change. The first day in the secondary school is a landmark in the process of growing up, from which they can happily despise the 'kids' school' they have just left. There are new subjects and more formal, more grown-up methods, enticing laboratories, craft rooms and gymnasia, and children get a sense of being part of a larger, more adult, more powerful organization.

But a big school and its unfamiliar ways can also be worrying and stifling. Some children may react happily to the new size and strangeness. Others may take time to adjust themselves. When we as adults go to a new job, we take time to get to know the customs, conventions and methods of the new firm. We talk about taking time to settle in. The same is true for children going to a new school. Getting the hang of a new and complicated timetable which involves finding one's way around a straggling and unfamiliar building is more than most of us have to do when we start a new job.

Many secondary schools take little or no trouble to make the transition easy. Their teachers may never even enter the primary schools from which their new pupils come, and some of them may charge ahead with new lessons careless of the fact that for some of the children the material may be boringly familiar and for others completely unknown. Of course, in some places primary school children are taken by their teachers to visit the new secondary school in the term before they are admitted to it, and then the teachers of the two schools are quite likely to consult each other about the curriculum, and it is also likely that a summary record card may go to the new school with the child transferred. But this is nowhere near common practice at present.

Nor are secondary schools at all ready to introduce themselves to new pupils and parents as an increasing number of primary schools do. Many local authorities do not even send parents a leaflet explaining secondary education, the choices open to parents or the courses which schools offer. So parents are very much more on their own here than they were when the children were five years old. In some ways the schools' attitude is a reflection of the children's. As they go into the secondary school children want to feel older and more independent. They do not want parents constantly fussing. Children still need the kind of support outlined in earlier chapters, but at the secondary stage it has to be less obtrusive. The next chapters will make this clearer. It is enough to say here that the transfer to secondary school can be thought of as a signal to parents to 'change gear' in their attitudes to schools and towards the older pupils their children are becoming.

8 The Secondary School Curriculum

When, by whatever method of transfer, your child at last gets to his secondary school, he will find it in many ways very different from the primary school he has just left. In the first place it will be a great deal bigger. Most primary schools have fewer than 300 pupils. Most secondary schools have more than this and some have 800 or 1,000. Comprehensive schools, in particular, tend to be large. Another difference is that the secondary school is as likely to be in a new building as not. Over half the children now in secondary schools are in buildings put up since the war, and something like one in five of them is in a school built since 1960. This is in marked contrast to the primary schools, though there is now a bias towards rebuilding old primary schools, and it means that many children going to a secondary school go to a new building from an old one.

But, though these differences of size and age are important, they are not what fundamentally distinguishes the secondary stage of education from the primary stage. To understand this we have to ask what secondary education is supposed to mean. As long ago as 1927 the official Hadow Report on secondary education was called 'the education of the adolescent', and it is worth seeing for a moment what this implies. Adolescence means the time of becoming an adult and it is a period of dramatic physical, mental and emotional changes – and secondary schools are designed to accommodate these. For example, at adolescence children become not only physically stronger but physically more competent and able to work to fine limits. So the secondary schools not only have playing fields for organized games and well-equipped gymnasia for physical education; they also have specialist rooms for art and craft and workshops for wood and metal-work. The child's emotional development also quickens at adolescence, so the teaching of history or English can come to involve the understanding of human motives and relation-ships. And, similarly, the capacity for logical thought which appears at adolescence encourages teachers to make learning a somewhat more systematic business and to introduce their pupils to a deeper understanding of science and scientific methods.

Becoming adult also means coming to terms with reality. Younger children often do not distinguish very well between fantasy and fact, but adolescence is a time of reconciling one's wants and imagination to the possibilities offered by the real world. This desire is very strong. It leads young people to demand that their school studies should be realistic or relevant to life. Indeed, most adolescents are anxious for specific pre-paration for jobs and careers. More and more schools are finding that it is best to build upon these interests of the children. Of course, the curriculum is not limited by the pupils' interests, but it does arise out of them; and it can mean that the blurring of subject boundaries which we notice in the primary school is rapidly spreading at the secondary stage.

Growing up also involves accepting responsibilities, and schools increasingly try to give their pupils experience in this. In fact, the choices they offer can be extremely important ones. Children are encouraged to choose their own courses, in the light of proper information about possibilities and con-sequences. And within the lessons themselves, the tendency to cut down on instruction and demonstration from the teacher and to increase experiment, research and writing up by pupils itself places upon them a growing responsibility for their own education.

How does all this work out in practice? The larger size of

the school means of course that children will have to be taught in a number of groups. If 200 children go up from a number of primary schools to a particular secondary school, they are almost bound to be divided into six 'forms' of thirty or more children in each. Your child will find himself in form 1A, 1B and so on and will probably find that he has a form room which acts as a base for his particular group and in which he has a desk for keeping his books, papers and instruments. This room will probably also be the headquarters of his 'form master' who will have some overall responsibility for the pupils in his form but may not actually teach them.

The way in which the children are divided into forms may vary from school to school. It may be done alphabetically or at random. But most often it is done by some measure of ability and in this case it is known as 'streaming'. In essence this means that the brightest children are put into form 1A, the next brightest into form 1B and so on down the alphabet. There is obviously a certain arbitrariness in this procedure, especially in the first year at secondary school. It may also be done on the basis of primary school records or by a test given to children early in the term. The argument for streaming is that if you have a class with thirty children of widely differing abilities it is very hard to teach them as a group. The bright ones will be wanting to push ahead. Those in difficulty will be lagging – and some will be neglected while the teacher goes at the pace of the majority. In other words, forms containing widely differing abilities handicap the teacher and penalize many of the children. Most teachers, certainly at the secondary stage, are in favour of streaming.

But there are some teachers who are against it. They argue that it is all a matter of the way you teach. If individual pupils can work at their own pace, groups of mixed ability create no difficulty. These teachers argue that streaming is very bad for the less bright children who may get demoralized and disaffected. They doubt very much whether bright children are really held back by being educated with the rest.

The argument is by no means settled yet, but the persistent minority against streaming appears to be growing.

One consequence of this is that even schools which do stream try to disguise the fact. Although they divide children by ability, they do not label them in alphabetical order starting with the brightest. They may instead label the forms after the initials of the teacher, so that Mr Young's form, which has the brightest children, may be form 1Y while Mrs Floud, who has the least bright children, will have 1F. Other schools stream, as it were, only at the top and bottom of the ability range; that is, they make up a form of the very brightest children and another form of those with some educational difficulty and then divide the rest at random. This means that most forms have a pretty wide range of ability, though without the very brightest or the least bright, and with two 'special' forms at each end. Schools which do this claim that it gives them the advantages of streaming without the disadvantages: most children, after all, are neither very bright nor very dull.

Putting a child into his appropriate form is of course not the end of organization of lessons in secondary schools. In his primary school your child was probably taught throughout the day by one teacher, with perhaps exceptions for subjects like music or handicraft. The systematized learning in the secondary school means that he is far more likely to be taught by different teachers for different subjects. Most teachers will be specialists teaching science or history or whatever it is to the different forms which come to them. The children, therefore, will move between specialist rooms from one lesson to another. This specialization normally leads schools to impose another division on top of the basic grouping into forms. The argument is that among children of very similar ability some may be good at mathematics, others at modern languages and so on. So for these subjects they are re-divided according to their ability in them. These groups are normally called 'sets'. Indeed, if the school has the staff to do so, there may be more sets in a year than there are forms, with of course fewer children in each. So your son may find himself in form 1D, in set 1.1 for modern languages (because he is good at French), in set 1.6 for science (because he is poor at that) and set 1.4 for mathematics (because he is average in it). Setting can also involve choice. As your child goes through the school he may be offered a choice between two languages or between two quite different subjects. There may, for example, be only one set in every year which does German – all the others doing French or Italian. Or it may even be that a child who wishes to do Latin may have to give up woodwork or art. Whatever his choice, he will find himself in the appropriate set. If all this seems a bit confusing on paper, you can take comfort from the fact that most children take to it without question in a day or two.

There is one other kind of division which schools employ which has little to do with ability or, indeed, with academic work at all. It relates instead to the size of secondary schools. We have already seen how pupils have form masters and specialist teachers. Most schools, however, see a need for something more than this and try to see that there is another member of staff with the responsibility for keeping an eye on the whole development and progress of each individual child. The most common way of doing this is through what is known as the 'house system' – because it derives from the actual residential houses of boarding schools. The house system can be somewhat artificial in day schools and may be most in evidence on sports days when the houses compete against each other. But a number of new schools are being built in which the houses have a physical base: each has its own dining room, cloakroom and so on. In most schools, however, the house system implies simply that groups of pupils of all ages may meet, say, once a week but are in any case the particular concern of house tutors who are ready to help and advise in personal as well as academic matters. In each house, too, the older pupils will be given responsibility for organization and usually for discipline.

It is not only the children, of course, who find themselves in many different groups – in a form, a set or a house. Each teacher, too, has a number of separate jobs – as a form master, a specialist teacher or a house tutor. And the senior teachers may have additional responsibilities, as heads of departments organizing the work in a particular subject throughout the school, or as house masters organizing the personal care of perhaps a quarter of the school. And above it all there is the head teacher who may seem somewhat remote, especially to younger pupils, but upon whom depends the atmosphere of the school, its attitude to work and the efficiency with which it operates.

So much for organization – but what is actually taught? Superficially at any rate many parents will find secondary school methods less puzzling than the primary stage. There has been no change in teaching methods comparable with that which has liberated primary school children from their rows of desks. On the other hand, different attitudes to education and to particular subjects are spreading fast, and perhaps the most startling development is in the sheer spread of knowledge which most children are now asked to cope with. It is not just that the highly academic courses leading to further and higher education are making ever more exacting demands; the curriculum of most children has also been broadened to include subjects which even ten years ago were thought beyond the grasp of all but a few. In particular this has meant the rapid spread of mathematics, science and modern languages.

Of course, the precise curriculum your child follows will depend upon the school he is at. Even with the demands of external examinations each school has considerable freedom, as does the individual teacher within each school. Similarly, the curriculum will depend to some extent upon the type of school to which your child goes. Leaving aside differences

in quality, a grammar school may offer a more academic
approach, a secondary modern school a more practical one.
A large comprehensive school may offer a wider range of
choice than either. Methods will vary too. Some secondary
schools will be recognizably the same as those which parents
themselves attended. Others will be strange and bewildering.
If this chapter concentrates on the latter it will be because it
is here that parents need most help. Some clues to what is
happening can be found in the knowledge of the way children
grow and develop and in the experience of primary schools
in adjusting their practices to meet this. In particular, education can no longer be divided rigidly into self-contained subjects; it arises most naturally from the interests of the pupils
themselves; and the pupils are given the initiative in their
own education. In the secondary schools the opportunities
for all this are greater because of the physical, mental and
emotional growth of pupils and their emergence as young
adults.

However much individual schools differ, there is a growing
feeling that there should be a basic content of secondary
education for all children. There are no longer regulations
which lay down what this should consist of, but the large
and unspoken agreement is that it should include mathematics, science and a foreign language as well as English, history,
physical education, arts, handicrafts and the rest. Increasingly,
teachers are accepting the obligation to offer the whole of this
broad curriculum to pupils, whatever their abilities. There
is obviously a limit to the extent to which all pupils can or
should follow the same course. What the schools do is to
create what they call a 'common core' of subjects which
all pupils take. Gradually, as they go through the secondary
school, they may choose additional subjects, drop subjects or
concentrate upon a group of subjects within the common
core. The object is to give them all a good all-round education
and then to encourage them to specialize in subjects studied
in greater depth. There have been persistent worries that

specialization is taking place too early. For most children the basic course clusters round English, social studies, science, mathematics, art and physical education; but towards the end of secondary school courses, between a third and a half of their time will be spent on specialist interests. A boy concentrating on English and social studies may find himself doing less science – and so on.

In all this the school tries to offer, not just a collection of isolated subjects, but a course which hangs together and to which all its separate parts constitute. The fashionable word is 'integrated', and it is expressed in a number of ways. In the first place the school may try to plan the secondary course as a whole. This means, for example, that teachers may have a different attitude from parents to the raising of the school-leaving age. Parents and pupils may think of this in terms of doing an extra year in school. Teachers, by contrast, feel it means replanning the whole course from the first year to the fifth in a new and coherent way. One must not overdo the idea of a continuous course. At each stage the material has to be suitable for the child's interests and state of development at the time. There is no sense in offering material whose usefulness will become clear only a year or two later. In the past a number of syllabuses simply spread the material of a particular subject over four years. Science, for example, began with the amoeba in the first form and reached man (if one was lucky) by the fourth. History similarly took the same time to go from the Stone Age to the nineteenth century. This sort of course may have looked coherent on paper but the sense of it may have escaped the pupils. These days the object is to see that the activities and methods of various disciplines are met and practised when the children are ready for them. In science, for example, the younger children may enjoy observing and classifying: the older will understand the controlled experiment, the hypothesis and the methods of logical thought. In history the younger children may again be concerned with stories or accounts of everyday life in the past:

the older ones will be concerned with evidence, purpose and motive.

In other words, the secondary course begins with the education of children but ends with the education of young adults. Coherently planned over the years of adolescence, it seeks to match at each step the developing potential of the pupils. Such a course begins to offer, perhaps for the first time in Britain, a preparation for life which aspires to being adequate.

A second way in which the course can be thought of as 'integrated', rather than as just a collection of subjects, is in the blurring of distinctions between subjects. This process has taken place to the greatest extent in some of the new primary schools, but as we shall see it is invading the secondary schools as well. If the secondary schools seem more resistant, it is partly because their teachers are specialists concerned with the integrity of their subjects and partly because the pupils are prepared for external examinations based upon the old subject divisions. But evidence for change is everywhere. It is not only that teachers are beginning to offer mathematics as a coherent discipline, rather than a collection of isolated techniques called arithmetic, algebra, geometry, trigonometry and so on: it is that old favourites like history and geography (for example) are coming together in a group of 'social studies', which may include disciplines like sociology, psychology and economics, which have hitherto had little place in schools. There is a similar movement in the sciences. In a sense the rest of this chapter is a discussion of the way this process is worked out in detail.

I have hinted that the variety in secondary schools makes possible, indeed encourages, a choice of curriculum. In primary schools all the children in a class follow the same syllabus as a matter of course. Within the overall syllabus, the teacher gives them the opportunity for individual initiative: they work at their own pace and follow their own interests. But in secondary schools this initiative is formalized. At various stages the children will be required to choose what course they take. A child may be asked to choose quite early on. In his second year, for example, he may be asked to decide whether to take a second language, or to choose one of two possible languages. In the third year he may be offered different kinds of science courses, one concentrating on the biological sciences, another on technology and so on. By the fourth year, the choices may be even more fundamental. A child may be asked to accept a particular bias for his own work. The divisions here are likely to be very broad: he will be offered what is basically a science course or an 'arts' course. (The latter means English, social studies, modern languages and so on.)

Even here, the attempt will be made to think of the course as a whole, not just as a collection of specialities. In particular, a number of teachers feel that children should be kept in touch with those areas of human knowledge which are remote from their special subjects. A child concentrating on the sciences is thought to need a humanizing contact with the arts. One specializing in social science needs to understand modern technology. There is a great deal of debate about how such a broadening of interest should be achieved, and it is fair to say that many teachers are baffled by the problem of 'integrating' what seem at first sight to be alien disciplines in a coherent if specialized course.

It is also true that there is much disquiet about the extent to which fundamental choices are made around the age of fourteen. One reason why it happens at that age is that schools tend to offer a two-year course leading to an external examination at the age of sixteen. But it is almost certainly too early for young people to make a rational decision on something which can affect their education for many years ahead and indeed their whole careers and lives. It is one of the prices we pay in Britain for the high priority we give to early academic attainment. This, and the competition for places in higher education, demands specialization. In these circumstances, the most the schools can do is to try to see that no decision is irrevocable, by keeping children in touch with key subjects in areas in which they are not specializing.

The Curriculum

Let us now see how all this works out in terms of the curriculum. Of course, we can't cover everything in half a chapter, but perhaps one can show how the principles of child development affect the practice of education in the schools – paying particular attention to those aspects which parents may find puzzling or unfamiliar.

As in the chapter on primary schools we begin with English. This, after all, is the subject which most parents are most concerned about. When a number of parents of fifteen-year-old school-leavers were asked what they thought were the most important things a school could teach, very nearly all of them said, 'To be able to put things in writing easily'. They are right in thinking that a good grasp of English is fundamental but this certainly often leads parents to complain that schools neglect English these days or teach it in airy-fairy ways which do not give a good grounding.

When most of us were at school English was a subject like any other, with specific things to learn in it. We learned not only that a noun was a naming word, but also that there was a difference between proper nouns (with capital letters) and common nouns (without). We could distinguish phrases and clauses, both adjectival and adverbial. For the more advanced there were gerunds or verbal nouns. And we were often asked to say, of words, what 'parts of speech' they were: we learned how to 'parse' sentences. At the same time we learned punctuation and did exercises in it. Some of us even came to understand the difference between a colon and a semi-colon. Many of us may even remember a teacher with a passion about commas and capital letters. Spelling was considered all-important. There were not only periodic tests and dictations –

but mistakes had to be corrected by writing the words correctly over and over again.

It is a common complaint among parents that in the new secondary schools, as in primary schools, this has all gone by the board. 'They don't teach them to spell any more' is a frequent complaint from parents and employers alike, and complaints about the standard of writing are even louder. One can take some of the complaints with a pinch of salt. Few parents keep their own old exercise books which would reveal the dreadful standards they themselves attained. Many of the most vociferous employers are those offering pay and conditions which no longer attract decently educated applicants. But there is observation in the complaint too. In secondary schools there *are* fewer formal lessons in grammar, spelling and punctuation. These are not ignored entirely. Your child's exercise book is still likely to have spelling and punctuation corrections. He will pick up the routine rude comments about neatness. But teachers of English no longer feel that any of this is an end in itself. They want their pupils' writing to be legible and the punctuation and spelling to help rather than hinder understanding. The quality of writing, spelling and punctuation, in other words, is an aid to communication. The teacher's main concern is with what is written, how it is expressed and whether it succeeds in its object. His long-term objective will be to enable pupils to listen and read with understanding, to speak and write fluently, clearly and creatively – and to go on doing this throughout life. (Doubting parents may ask themselves quietly how often they have turned to the elaborately acquired grammar of their school-days.)

The point about all this is that the English language is not so much a subject to be learned as a tool to be used, to gain understanding and to communicate with others. Often teachers in secondary schools begin, as parents begin with young children and as the infant schools do, with speech. This is our most natural means of expression, and the schools are beginning to bring speech back into the curriculum, not to embark upon the arrogant task of 'improving' pupils' accents but to give them the greatest possible practice in expressing themselves. This is why pupils are encouraged to talk with their teachers and with one another, to listen and be listened to, to debate and discuss, to improvise dramatic scenes and so on. It is why oral tests and examinations, for all their drawbacks, are being reintroduced. English education has traditionally neglected speech. So much so that people who can speak fluently are both envied and distrusted. But an education which leaves pupils tongue-tied is no education at all.

Speech, then, is the most natural way to communicate, and we have come to think of reading and writing as almost equally natural extensions of it. The secondary schools assume that their pupils already have the basic skills. What they try to do is to give children practice, in ways which change with their changing interests, capacities, emotions and understanding. The kind of things they read and write will be quite different at the beginning and end of their secondary school days.

Most people read either for information or for pleasure, and the schools desire to give pupils the ability to do both effectively. For example, it is not just that a complicated society depends on people being able to read – to understand notices, fill up forms and master instructions, to discover what is happening in the country and the world, to learn a new subject, master a new trade or skill or take up a hobby. It is that for most things we have to make decisions – about buying one product rather than another, about choosing a holiday, about voting at an election. We read for information certainly – but we also need to be able to read critically. We want to ask what is this advertisement or that politician really saying? Are the promises quite what they seem? So secondary school children are taught not only to read, not only to mop up information, but to ask 'Is this true?' – or 'Does this set out to inform or mislead?' A great deal of the work of a secondary school English course is designed to assist the critical spirit in the acquisition of knowledge.

But reading is not just about information. It is also an entertainment and, more importantly, a means of growing in understanding. Reading may amuse or kill time. It may also shock, disgust or irritate. It can make us think and introduce us to new ideas; can arouse our imaginations and introduce us to worlds which we would otherwise never meet. It enlarges not only our information but our experience and our understanding. We can learn from the situations in stories and poetry as well as we can learn from our own personal lives. Some parents get impatient with the study of literature in schools and cannot see why children spend their time on novels about people from the past or on poetry which is remote from reality. But literature and poetry are about people acting in particular situations and reacting to each other. They are about feelings and emotions. Through them children can learn about themselves, about other people, about personal relationships, about opportunities and frustrations, about social pressures and about what constitutes vice or virtue. So a good part of the secondary school English curriculum will be devoted to the study of stories, novels and poems – and the basic purposes of this remain even when the exercise is directed towards an examination where the mugging up of detail may come to seem more important than the enlarging of experience.

But being educated is not just a matter of absorbing experience, either at first or second hand. This essentially passive notion is one of the casualties of modern methods. No longer are children in school regarded in the light of the schoolroom in Dickens's *Hard Times* – 'the inclined plane of little vessels then and there arranged in order, ready to have imperial gallons of facts poured into them until they were full to the brim'. Learning is now thought of in terms of doing. It is more effective as well as more blessed to give than to receive.

This means that writing is thought of as being quite as educative as reading. This idea often puzzles parents. They may regard writing as something which is mainly 'useful' – for letters, job applications and jotting down notes. They find it hard to see that writing helps you to understand things. But perhaps most authors write, not so much to make themselves understood, as to help themselves to understand. Putting a thing down on paper is an essential part of learning. In an important sense it is only when we have expressed something ourselves that we can be said to have mastered it. Similarly, it is hard to see how we can be said to be thinking unless we have put things into words. The better command we have of words the better our command of ideas.

So children in secondary schools get practice in reading, certainly, but also practice in writing, and the thing to remember is that writing is an essential part of the learning process. It is not just a way of showing the teacher what they have learned. Children's writing in secondary schools is not just a matter of presenting facts. Their writing is about themselves, their experiences, their family, friends and interests. And though they may start with these immediate concerns, they do not stop there: they use them as a basis for further exploration of the world. They explore not only the facts but the world of emotion, morals and imagination. Some of the most convincing evidence of the way in which this approach stretches the capabilities of children can be found in the many anthologies of children's work now available. But better still, if you seek to be convinced, try to see what is done in your child's school, not least by your own children.

As with English, parents may find themselves as bothered with mathematics at the secondary as at the primary stage. Our difficulties are even enhanced by the fact that this may have marked the moment of our own failure. Our greater insecurity may hinder understanding of what the schools are now doing. At a pinch we might have brought ourselves to face the old enemy. To find him now changed out of recognition is often too much. The clue to the new ideas lies in what we have been saying about the whole of secondary education: that its tendency is to centre round problems rather than subjects. In the past it was unquestionably assumed that one tackled mathematics in a definite order, beginning with simple arithmetic. Only those who had shown the greatest proficiency in this could manage the other distinct branches of mathematics like algebra, geometry and trigonometry. These branches usually had quite distinct syllabuses, taught in different periods, often by different people – and rarely if ever did one discover any connection between them. What they all had in common was their method of instruction. You were given a formula and you applied it. 'Put down the 3 and carry 1' we muttered to ourselves or 'Bring down the next figure from the divisor.' Or '$(a + b)^2 = a^2 + 2ab + b^2$' and 'The square on the hypotenuse of a right-angled triangle is equal to the sum of the squares on the other two sides.' What we did was to learn the formula and apply it. At the end of every chapter of our textbooks were pages of exercises which we worked our way through.

Of course, there are plenty of schools where these methods continue. There are still teachers who defend them, arguing that the formulae and their manipulation form the basis of mathematics, which have to be mastered before anything else can be added. It is a common view that learning anything demands, first of all, a period of drudgery: a subject's interest reveals itself only later on. Of course, every activity in school, as elsewhere, involves a large measure of routine – but there is nothing dull about mathematics and there is no excuse for making it so.

There were other objections, too, to the old mathematics with which parents had more sympathy. The main one was its remoteness from reality. There is a moment in *How Green was my Valley*, by Richard Llewellyn, in which a school-boy is struggling with a problem of the rate at which a bath will be filled if the water is running in at one speed and out at another – to which his mother very reasonably observed that only a fathead would try and fill a bath in such circumstances. Many people have discovered for the first time, long after leaving school, the meaning of some process they had spent years repeating. It was not just that they came to see the application of what they had been doing (though it seems a long time to have waited even for that) but that they understood it for the first time.

The educational objection to the old methods was that they did not do what they claimed to do. They did not give people a good grounding. They were trying, in fact, to do something too difficult too early. They were too abstract, giving children a formula and making them practise it. They presented the children with the most difficult part first. What we know about child development suggests that thinking in abstract terms is something that comes late for children, perhaps mainly at adolescence. What they can grasp is the reality which the formulae express. For this reason it is often best to introduce shapes and volumes (what used to be called geometry, or worse still solid geometry) before much of the traditional arithmetic. I am not quite sure which was the more depressing: the large number of children who never mastered the formulae at all or the more 'successful' ones who learned them happily, manipulated them perfectly and never understood what they were doing.

The new methods are grounded in a belief that mathematics is a language which enables you to say things you cannot say in other ways. It is another way of looking at things, of understanding and solving problems. Learning mathematics the old way was like being given a message to deliver in a language you did not understand. You could, with application, memorize the message and repeat it faithfully when required, but it did not teach you anything, and if anybody responded to it you were left speechless. The new mathematics seeks to give pupils, above all, understanding. It does this in a number of ways. The most obvious is that what were formerly regarded as academic problems – like simple and compound interest – are now related to practical matters like budgeting, fitting out a home, hire purchase, travel and the like. Pupils can see the point of their calculations when these help them to understand the significance (for example) of paying interest in hire purchase on the whole sum over the period of a loan. And they will be thinking differently about everything in their daily lives, thinking more precisely and more rationally.

This sort of change need not create too much difficulty for parents: they may even welcome it. Those schools which have taken the new mathematics furthest are trying to do much more than this, to abolish fear and distrust and extend their pupils' creative abilities. One example of their ways of doing this has become familiar through some television programmes. You and I are used to counting in tens. All our school sums were done in terms of hundreds, tens and units. But we don't have to count in tens, and the television example points out that an octopus (having eight tentacles rather than ten fingers and thumbs) would be likely to count in eights. Computers, it is added, count in twos. By the time we have counted up to 9 we have run out of units, so our next figure has to be one ten and no units. We write it 10 (one-nought). If we are counting in eights, we can get up to seven before running out of units: the next figure has to be one eight and no units and is also written 10 (one-nought). To put it technically, 10 in the base eight is the same as 8 in the base ten. We can add, subtract, multiply and divide in any base we like. The point is that a child who is used to counting in different bases is unlikely to be intimidated by numbers. He can make them do what he wants them to do, and those of us who can only marvel at him may envy his confidence.

Perhaps all this makes clear some of the unfamiliar features of your child's new mathematics textbook. If you open it, you will see that there are no obvious divisions along the old lines between arithmetic, algebra and geometry. One page may remind you of geometry and another of algebra. Some pages may have arithmetic, algebra and geometry all mixed up. And some pages may have the quite unfamiliar symbols of formal logic. None of this will puzzle your child, to whom with any luck one symbol may be quite as unsurprising as another. Another thing you may notice is that the book will be trying to make visible the abstract ideas of mathematics, so that every page will be filled with pictures and diagrams. A third difference from the textbook you yourself remember may be that you will find it hard to discover separate pages of exposition, followed by pages of examples to be worked out. The exposition will itself be couched in terms of problems. The child will be required to think from the start, answering questions as he goes along – and coming to the formula (if at all) only after he understands the basis for it. The book will help the children themselves to discover the facts and principles of mathematics. The line between instruction and repeated practice is scarcely visible.

The changes that are taking place in English and mathematics are paralleled in other branches of the curriculum. For example, in science the old subject divisions between physics, chemistry and biology are breaking down. There is much less emphasis on demonstration by the teacher followed by copying up notes and much more on discovery and experiment by pupils. The syllabus may typically start not with the formulation of laws and principles but with the pupils' own experience. To take only one example, a science syllabus might centre round human biology. This in itself makes a change, since in the past children often began with the amoeba or some such creature and approached the functioning of their own bodies tentatively, if at all. In human biology, children learn about the body's structure and function and about its various parts and organs. They follow the cycle of human life from conception to death and come to understand the principles of growth and development, the mechanisms of heredity. From this they come to understand the requirements of health and hygiene. In this, of course, the children are moving away from pre-occupation with individual human beings and are coming to study social arrangements – in this case for public health. Similarly, in studying the senses, they move on to understand the science of behaviour and learning. From this they may go on to look at man in his environment in various parts of the world in the past, the present and even in the future. Such a syllabus can be seen to involve not only human biology but chemistry, psychology, sociology, anthropology, but all related to a central interest of young people – themselves.

Even so, the biology of man might be only the central core of studies in science. A teacher might lead out from it in many directions. One might be into the study of all living things, to show the nature and variety of life and the way in which man, animals and plants are interdependent. This part of the syllabus might encourage a respect for living things and an interest in the conservation of wild life and the countryside. It might show the application of biology in agriculture. In another direction, human biology might be the start of studies in understanding the continuity of life through the theory of evolution. In yet another, studies of the human environment might lead to work on the earth and its place in the universe. A few schools are also going on to show how man extends his limited capacities through the use of machines and engines. Here children not only learn about the sources, forms and measurement of energy, about light and sound, and about the nature, development and uses of materials: they also go on to the practical application of this, so that technology enters the curriculum as well as science.

Such a syllabus would obviously cover a number of the familiar scientific subjects, like chemistry, physics, astronomy, mathematics, mechanics and geology. However, these subjects are not presented in isolation, but as parts of a coherent attempt to understand the nature of man and the world.

In modern languages, too, the emphasis is on the use of the skill of communication. As with English studies, it is not that teachers have suddenly decided that grammar is unimportant but that they have come to prize understanding and fluency – which the grammar can be seen to support at the appropriate stage. There is inevitably a good deal of grammar in the teaching of languages, but teachers these days try to see that, after five years of learning French, their pupils can at least get themselves a cup of coffee in a café in Boulogne.

In all this change, one of the problems which parents face is that the names for aspects of the curriculum seem to keep changing too. For example, many parents are puzzled by a topic called 'social studies'. If they enquire about it they may realize that its material would look familiar if it were called history or geography. But the change of name is not arbitrary. It does represent the attempt to give coherence and relevance to what is taught. Of course, in some schools the change will be in the name alone, but in the brighter places it will represent a new way of looking at old subjects. The study of man in different circumstances from one's own – in the past or in different parts of the world – is an important aid to understanding. It is, however, increasingly hard to understand modern society in these terms alone. Teachers find themselves introducing new disciplines like economics (the study of industrialized society), psychology (the science of human behaviour) and sociology (the study of people in groups). A fully developed social studies course will include elements of all these disciplines, even if it starts in a homely fashion with the immediate neighbourhood or town. And it may have the advantage that it involves the children themselves in exploring and investigating: with a little less of a trudge through a textbook accompanied by the writing up of notes, a little more of the methods of personal research and project work.

On top of all this there is in many schools today a richness of provision for those subjects outside the academic curriculum which many parents can find astonishing and impressive. The equipment for physical education and games, the music rooms with the provision of instruments, the expansion of the familiar art rooms of the past to include studios for pottery, carving, printing, bookmaking and so on, the workshops and domestic science 'flats', all serve to extend a child's capacity and imagination by helping him to create, perform, fashion materials and plan constructively. What this provision symbolizes is a change from the attitude that music and other arts and crafts were a 'frill' to a serious curriculum – or a consolation prize for those who were good at nothing else – to one which regards the nurturing of creative ability and imaginative achievement as a central function of education.

This has been a pretty brisk trot through the curriculum of modern secondary schools. What I have tried to do is to show what attitudes are behind it, so that parents faced with some unfamiliar activity may be able to set this in context. Of course, a summary like this must give the impression of something rather ideal. Many schools cannot live up to the promise of their methods. Admirable attitudes can falter in practice. Large numbers of schools are in any case untouched by modern methods, even in aspiration. But these schools on the whole will be comprehensible to parents. Strangeness comes when a school is not resting on its laurels but is trying something different. On the whole parents can welcome unfamiliarity as evidence of life and thought.

In all these changes, parents may come across a certain amount of educational jargon which is at first sight bewildering. One of the commonest phrases is 'curriculum development'. This simply implies a certain amount of organization for experiment and change. Teachers, with any luck, may often introduce new ideas in their teaching. There are also a lot of organizations which exist to promote such changes. There is the Schools Council for the Curriculum and Examinations, which is sponsoring the writing of textbooks, the preparation of material and the creation of courses, which are all assessed by experts, tried out in selected schools, revised and assessed again before they are made available to schools in general. The Nuffield Foundation has sponsored a large number of experiments like this in secondary as well as in primary schools. Here again, 'Nuffield science' simply means that your child's school is using materials prepared in this way with the support of the Foundation.

Another common phrase is 'educational technology'. This means gadgets. Schools are increasingly using film strips, films, television, including closed-circuit television, radio and all manner of other devices. The most formidable to look at (though not necessarily educationally most successful) is the language laboratory – in which individual pupils sit in booths wearing headphones and working tape recorders in order to practise the use of a modern language. Teaching machines – which are elaborate devices based upon simple learning theory – may also be available. The theory – which can be expressed in books quite as well as on machines – is often known as 'programmed learning'. In effect this breaks down what has to be learned into very small steps in which mastery of one leads on to the next.

Another phrase which parents may come across is 'team teaching'. The phrase is American, the practice on the whole is English. In secondary schools, we are quite used to the idea of specialist teachers for different subjects. In this sense the teachers in a school are a 'team'. In theory the notion can be carried further by organizing the teachers' work more flexibly. For example, one teacher may be giving a basic lecture to a very large number of pupils, while others are dealing with individual difficulties in small groups – rather than having each teacher facing the normal class of thirty pupils all the time.

There will no doubt be other fads and fancies, some describing real innovation, others merely new names for old practices. If some jargon puzzles you, ask a teacher about it. This will help to reduce reverence both for the jargon and for the teacher.

To Leave School or Not

About half the children in the country leave school at the earliest possible opportunity, and about half the rest do so a year later. The school-leaving age was raised to sixteen in 1972, and it is not quite clear what effect this raising of the age will have on subsequent staying on. The general arguments for and against staying on at school can be put very simply. Children stay at school because they enjoy it and because they or their parents calculate that it will help them to get a better job, perhaps after even further education and training. Children leave school because they are fed up or because they or their families need the money which they can earn if they go straight into employment. On the economic side, the calculation which they have to make is this: will the increased earnings which I am likely to get during my lifetime, in the better job which further education makes available to me, compensate for the loss of earnings as a teenager? In general, the evidence is that extra education not only compensates for loss of earnings but produces a positive benefit over a person's lifetime. Of course, what happens to individuals may differ widely. There are plenty of those who have stayed at school but have not earned well throughout their lives. This is why you might let the general rule affect your attitude to staying on: your particular decision will be based on what you know about the individual child. Of course, job satisfaction depends on more than the amount of money it brings. But here the argument for additional education is equally strong. What it tends to bring is choice of job. The less education you have the less you are able to choose what you will do.

There are a number of reasons why pupils may get fed up with school. It may be just the general restlessness of adolescence, the need for novelty and change. This may be exacerbated by personal difficulties, such as a dislike of a particular teacher or frustration at not being able to get a course one wants. These personal difficulties are bound to arise, and although they can be mitigated by understanding on the part of parents and teachers, they may loom so large to the individual pupil that he becomes determined to leave. Many adolescent pupils get increasingly dissatisfied with school as school. They resent being in the same institution as eleven-year-olds. They feel that they should be treated more as adults. Some schools make matters worse here by insisting on petty regulations, particularly about dress, but even those with more liberal attitudes to uniform have to allow for the fact that they accommodate younger children alongside the older ones. One might add that the general loosening of respect for authority makes some young people reject the idea of becoming prefects and accepting responsibility in the upper school.

Pupils and parents may have a quite different view of what school is for from that held by the teachers. This in itself can create dissatisfaction. Pupils may find school increasingly remote from their needs and irrelevant to their main concerns. In particular they may feel that the school has too little to do with the practical needs of day-to-day life, especially with the business of getting a job and earning a living. This feeling is often strongest among those whose families, or indeed whose whole social background, act on the assumption that they will be out earning money as soon as possible. To a family living on the average industrial wage the extra money which a school-leaver can bring in makes a very significant difference. It is hard to see that there can be any gain from giving it up, especially when academic study seems to have no bearing on practical affairs.

These, then, are some of the reasons why pupils and their parents get dissatisfied with school. If it wants to keep pupils, the school may react in two ways. It may try to make its curriculum more practically biased and it may put the arguments for staying on in economic terms. But, of course, the school itself may not try to keep the pupil. It may feel that he is not sufficiently able, or that he has become too awkward. Despite all the changes that have been made in the curriculum for older pupils it is probably true that most schools still regard what they offer as something which pupils should earn by success, or at least show that they are capable of benefiting from. There is a largely unconscious rejection process at work which makes the schools struggle less determinedly to retain large numbers of pupils. This means that the school itself creates its own social pressures. If your child is at one where most pupils stay on, he too is likely to stay: if not, he probably won't. When it comes to staying on, the question is often resolved without much difficulty, indeed without much thought. Where the school expects pupils to stay, where parents accept the need for it and where pupils are relatively content, the pupils may stay almost without question, carried along on the escalator of middle-class values. Where a family needs money and most young people in the neighbourhood earn early, and where the school judges (perhaps rightly) that there is not much it can do for unruly adolescents, then the pupil will leave, probably to perpetuate the social deprivation of his own childhood. But there are families and pupils for whom things are not so simple. Working-class parents may suddenly find themselves faced with a child who wants to continue at school and is powerfully abetted by the school itself. Middle-class parents may equally suddenly find a child questioning all their assumptions and wishing to leave school as early as possible. A school may find itself constantly trying to persuade both pupils and their parents about the value of an extended education.

What should one say to parents who feel that the school is not offering very much and that it is time their teenage child was out earning? I do not underestimate the strength of the parents' case. From their point of view the school may well be a waste of time and the children are young adults who ought to be earning. If staying on at school is rare in a neighbourhood, it is the parents who have to take on the burden of rejecting the normally accepted social behaviour. Strongest of all is the financial argument. It is not only the very poor who feel the need of the earnings of their older children. Against all this, the arguments of educators can sound rather thin. They have to be couched in terms of the future – and the likely future at that. They deal in probabilities and opportunities, not with anything so tangible as a weekly wage packet. There are perhaps two ways of meeting this situation. The first is to make clear to parents the financial help they can get if their children do stay on. Unfortunately local authorities vary a good deal in the amount of help that they give. Some are relatively generous; others are mean. But parents should discover from the school what help they can get, if money is tight, and they should have no hesitation in applying for it if they qualify. The sort of grant you can get is for clothing and equipment. Equally, parents should remember to put into the financial calculation the loss of cheaper school dinners, cheaper fares and family allowance for the second and subsequent children and tax allowances where appropriate. These will obviously not add up to the total wage if the child takes a job, but many parents may be surprised to find that the difference is less than they thought. And it is, after all, the *difference* which is important: you have to ask yourself if the extra money the child brings in is absolutely crucial.

The second way one can answer parents who want children to leave is to persuade them that, even if the child leaves school, he need not leave education altogether. Parents who are unconvinced by the contribution of schools are often more impressed by vocational and other training courses. Even here the schools can help. If their own courses can be seen to be relevant to later life they will find it easier to convince doubting parents. But if the schools fail to 'sell' their own courses, they can at least point out to parents what is available in local technical colleges and colleges of further education. They can collaborate with the youth employment services to suggest jobs which carry an element of further education and training. The idea of apprenticeship, or learning a trade, can often be more attractive to parents than simply staying on at school, and it is up to the school to make these opportunities known. Unfortunately, many schools are ignorant about such things and unsympathetic to what the further education colleges have to offer. If the school is not much help, make the most of any interview with the Youth Employment Officer that may be made available. Try to make sure that the jobs for which your child is applying carry the possibility of release from work during the day to take further education and training. Get the prospectus of the local college and see the range of courses it has to offer in the evenings as well as during the day.

A similar approach is possible to parents who want a child to stay on when the child is reluctant to do so. This can so easily get into a wrangle about what the child will or will not do. If parents can accept, indeed offer, alternative possibilities, the child may feel that the pressure is off and agree to stay on at school anyway. But there is no reason why we should not respect the reasons which an adolescent gives for rejecting the school and its atmosphere. These are detailed earlier – and they are all entirely understandable. Many of them can be met by suggesting that the child continues his education in a local authority technical college. This need not mean taking technical courses. A large number of adolescents do continue their academic education in the colleges. One in five of all the candidates for G.C.E. O and A levels are in the colleges. They are there because the young people prefer the more adult atmosphere of the college – they are treated as students rather than as pupils – or because the college can offer them subjects which are not available at school. You will find all manner of students whose earlier schools were for some reason unable to offer A level courses, girls from posh boarding schools, students from small grammar schools, others from secondary moderns with no sixth forms, yet others from comprehensive schools which had not built up a wide enough range of courses. So if your child wants to leave school because he wants to leave *school* but retains an interest in his academic subjects; or if he wants to take a range of courses which the school cannot offer; or if he just wants a *change* – then think very seriously about the local tech. Many a parent has been astonished by the difference which this change makes at the age of sixteen.

Perhaps an example of this may help. A child may have struggled rather at school and may be thought likely to get a rather unimpressive result in C.S.E. or G.C.E. O level. The school may suggest that he is not up to A level work and will offer perhaps non-examination courses for a year after the school-leaving age. The child may feel that he does not want to continue his unimpressive performance and that the non-examination courses are an unattractive second best. It would be absurd, in my view, to argue that such a child should stay at school. Far better suggest that he goes to the local tech and takes A levels there. The atmosphere will be different. The child himself may be better motivated: he will be trying to prove the school's judgement wrong. He will be able to concentrate on his chosen subjects without the distraction of the rest of school life. He may well get his three A levels, one of them perhaps in one year, where the school had decided that he was unlikely to manage any. There is no need to overstate the case: most pupils taking A levels take them in school, but the case I have just described is very common, and more parents should know of the possibility.

But, of course, the technical college will offer very much more than A levels. If it is vocational relevance which the child is after, he will find an enormous range of possibilities there. There may be short courses leading to immediate qualification in, for example, shorthand or hairdressing. There are other courses associated with apprenticeships or jobs requiring training. There are others, full-time or part-time, which are in effect a route, taking several years, to the highest qualifications. If the objection that a child has to school is that he wants to be out earning money, then a parent may find that a part-time course, taken by young workers, is the answer. This is not the place to detail the range of opportunity available. Even students who go to the tech may not be entirely aware of it. This may explain the paradox that, although most of the children over the age of sixteen who get any education at all are getting it not in schools but in technical colleges, the work of the colleges is generally much less well known than that of the schools.

The Sixth Form

Those pupils who do stay on at school after sixteen are said to be in the 'sixth form', divided into the first- and second-year sixth. Traditionally they have followed a two-year course leading to G.C.E. A level (see later), which has been dominated by the demands of university entrance – even though most pupils were probably not going on to university. The schools themselves have always made a sharp distinction between the sixth form and what is often called 'the main school'. The distinction arises from the nature of the sixth form. First, it is composed entirely of pupils who are at school voluntarily. This affects their own attitudes to work and those of their teachers. Sixth-form work is largely 'academic'. Typically the course involves concentrated study 'in depth' of a relatively restricted range of subjects. This narrowness is defended educationally on the ground that it makes possible a thoroughness and attention to detail which characterizes the academic approach, and practically on the ground that university entry standards can be reached only by single-minded concentration. In the sixth form, too, pupils are encouraged to be more responsible for their own work. They not only very largely choose the subjects they will study, but a large part of their work will be done not in formal lessons but privately.

In other words, the sixth-former has a good deal more control over the amount and kind of work that he does than has a pupil in the main school or even than some university students. Traditionally, this sense of responsibility has been extended not only to the management of academic work but to sharing the organization and running of the school. The senior pupils may take on all manner of jobs as head of a house, a school prefect, as chairman of a school group or society or captain of a school team. To the more junior pupils of the school, a sixth-former may seem quite as much a part of the establishment as the staff.

Like so many things in schools, the sixth forms are changing. The most obvious way is in broadening the kind of courses that are offered. More pupils are staying on for other reasons than to take G.C.E. A level. Since the school-leaving age was raised to sixteen, it was expected that more and more pupils will stay on for non-academic courses. This is already familiar in some girls' schools because there have been several recognized professions for girls which recruited at eighteen without insisting on A level, so shorthand and typing, pre-nursing courses and the like have been introduced for girls pursuing their education after sixteen.

Another spur to change in the sixth form is that the schools are responding to new demands from their pupils. Young people over sixteen may no longer be content to work in the same atmosphere and organization as eleven-year-olds. Indeed, the fact that a school accommodates both younger and older pupils makes some pupils wish to leave. So the schools have given a great deal of thought to the creation of a more adult atmosphere for sixth-formers. In some schools this has meant giving the sixth-formers a separate block or wing of a building to themselves in which they may have a common room, library, study rooms and so on. Some of the more Victorian rules about uniform are being relaxed and some schools are even accepting the growing distaste among sixth-formers for the exercise of authority over younger children.

In a very few areas these thoughts about the sixth form have led to the establishment of quite separate 'sixth-form colleges'.

Examinations

Almost all schools have tests or examinations. They have them for their own purposes, but these are often shared by parents. Both teachers and parents, for example, feel the need to check periodically how much children are actually learning. With the more informal methods in the schools parents may particularly need to be assured that learning is taking place at all. Equally teachers need to be able to compare the achievement of one pupil with another. They may want to do this for setting or streaming. Again, parents are interested in knowing, not only that their child is learning and making progress, but how he compares with other children of his own age or in the same class. They want to know whether he is bright for his age or seems to be meeting some particular difficulty. So both teachers and parents accept the need for some sort of measure, in the form of a test.

Both parents and teachers also feel that tests are an important educational incentive. Children are naturally competitive and so may seek to do better if there is some way of deciding who has done best. Parents in particular may feel that the new methods in schools are all very well and that it may be ideal for children to learn because of the basic fascination of a subject: they also know that natural interest may be very short-lived and suspect that most children need the external pressure to learn that an examination provides. Both parents and the public at large also have a right to the assurance that the schools are doing their job. To a very large extent we have to take the schools' word for it, but we feel more secure if the schools can offer some recognizable and formal measure of what their pupils are achieving.

On the other hand, there are a number of good arguments

against tests, which a parent may best recognize when his own child is in some difficulty. Most tests are extremely crude. Their very form – that of answering a number of questions in a limited time – means that the things which are tested may be quite trivial. Most tests measure memory and that speed of reaction which people call intelligence. But these may not be the most important things about education. One disillusioned educator has said that what school tests usually measure is the ability to answer trivial problems quickly and accurately, whereas what life demands is the ability to tackle important problems with care and (most important) to learn from our mistakes.

Parents are also familiar with the criticism that an examination may come to dominate the curriculum. Ideally the test should reveal what has been taught and learned. What often happens is that the examination determines what is taught, and this can make the syllabus remote from the needs of the pupils. It can also determine teaching methods, encouraging mere memory at the expense of understanding and practice.

Nor is it very clear what most examinations actually measure. Parents will be familiar with the fact that one child, with a retentive memory and a quick grasp of new material, may sail through an examination for which another child may have to prepare with great effort. If both children get the same mark, a parent may well ask what the result has told us. Is a high degree of superficial facility equal to a high degree of concentration?

These dilemmas about examinations are bad enough when they are 'internal' examinations set by the schools themselves. Here there is a good chance that the examinations can arise naturally from the needs of teaching and of the pupils. The dilemmas are sharpened when the examinations are 'external' ones, set by some body outside the school. The external examinations may give pupils, parents, and the rest of us some national standard by which education can be measured, but they may come to dominate the curriculum rather than serve it.

Almost all children take internal tests and examinations. Fewer take external ones. Half of our children leave school at the earliest possible moment after the school-leaving age, which until now has been fifteen. This means that they have not even considered the major external examinations which are normally taken at sixteen. If they met public examinations at all they did so in the courses taken after school, which are normally part-time and lead to vocational qualifications. In the school year beginning in September 1972, the leaving age was raised to sixteen, and one of the very interesting questions is whether this will of itself lead to a lot more children taking examinations at what will then be the school-leaving age.

THE CERTIFICATE OF SECONDARY EDUCATION

The Certificate of Secondary Education (C.S.E.) is relatively new: it started in the summer of 1965. It was constructed specifically to meet many of the objections to examinations. In the first place its governing councils, examination committees and subject planning committees in its fourteen regional examining bodies all have a majority of teachers from schools affected by the examination. What is more, the examination has three 'modes' of operation, offering teachers a choice of initiatives. In the first mode schools submit their candidates for the regional examining board's examinations. In the second, schools or groups of schools put up their own examination schemes which are approved and set by the boards. In the third, the examinations are set and marked internally by individual schools or groups of schools, and these are moderated by the boards. This third mode obviously gives teachers the most freedom: they can meet the needs of their pupils directly with what is, in effect, an internal examination. On the other hand, pupils, teachers, parents and employers have the assurance about standards that an external examination gives. Only one in ten of all C.S.E. entries are for this mode, so clearly teachers have not yet gained sufficient confidence to run their own examinations directly.

C.S.E. is a subject examination. That is, you can get a certificate with only one subject on it, and there is no limit to the subjects you can offer. You don't have to pass a specific number or a specific combination of subjects before you get a certificate. There is no rigid pass or fail line in C.S.E., though the disguise of failure is not impenetrable. Results are given for each subject in five grades (1 to 5) or are ungraded. Grade 4 is, as it were, the average: it is meant to suggest a standard to be expected of a sixteen-year-old of average ability who has conscientiously pursued an appropriate course in the subject. Obviously pupils who get a grade higher than 4 are held to have done better than this: they may have higher ability or have been more conscientious. Grade 1 is meant to be comparable with the Ordinary level of the General Certificate of Education (see below). For those less successful than the average, grade 5 is meant to show that the candidate performed well enough to confirm that it was right for him to enter for the examination, but not well enough to reach the standard of our conscientious average sixteen-year-old. Candidates who do not qualify for grade 5 are ungraded – and the implication is that they were really not up to standard.

Your child will get a Certificate of Secondary Education if he can put on it more than one grade between 1 and 4. If he gets nothing but grade 5, in however many subjects, he does not get a certificate. On the other hand, if he does get a certificate, any grade 5 he gets is entered on it. All candidates are told their results, including ungradings, but these notices are not the same as a certificate.

The examination is thought to be suitable for a very wide range of ability from the most able (where it overlaps with G.C.E.) to those of just below average ability. This still leaves nearly half the age-group without a nationally recognized school-leaving qualification.

One important innovation which has followed the introduction of C.S.E. is the extension of the examination to subjects other than the traditional academic ones: examples of this are building and engineering science, civics and typewriting. In the past the less academic pupil may have been deterred from pursuing his studies in school by the fact that he might not do well in the academic examination at the end of the course. Now he can take C.S.E., and if he does well enough to get grade 1 can use this as a springboard to further his education at school, college or university.

GENERAL CERTIFICATE OF EDUCATION

The General Certificate of Education (G.C.E.) is the most familiar examination to those parents who themselves went to grammar schools or the like. G.C.E. was established in its present form in 1951. It replaced the old General School Certificate and Higher School Certificate examinations, and the replacement brought a significant change. The old examinations demanded passes in specific groups of subjects, and if pupils did not have the required number and combination of these they did not get a certificate. G.C.E., like C.S.E. later, was set up as a 'subject' examination: a pupil gets a certificate recording the passes he has attained regardless of how many there are. Some parents object that this destroys the value of the certificate. What good is a piece of paper with only one pass on it? They feel that the old demand for a specific number of subjects guaranteed a general education. On the other hand, it seems clearly better for a child to achieve something in one subject than in none and to have this achievement recognized. Even one subject may represent a qualification to an employer or for admission to a course in a technical college or elsewhere. The change was made to give the schools more flexibility and to offer incentive to a wider range of studies. It did not seem sensible to withhold recognition of one achievement just because somebody had not gained another.

For those who worried that the change meant a drop in standards, there was the comfort that the standard of the examination was in fact raised. The old School Certificate had three grades of award: pass, credit and distinction. The pass mark in the G.C.E. is comparable with the credit of the School Certificate. Since the change vastly more children are in fact achieving the old certificate standards.

The G.C.E. examination is held at two levels: Ordinary – O level – and Advanced – A level. O level comes at sixteen and A level at eighteen. But candidates may enter for different subjects at different dates and may enter for the same subject more than once. They can build up a number of subjects on their certificate over a number of years. In some schools pupils ignore O level altogether in the subjects which they are going to take at A level.

Passes at A level are graded A to E in descending order of merit and those who do not get a grade may be awarded an O level pass if their performance warrants it. Candidates at A level in a particular subject may attempt special papers in it. Passes are not awarded in these papers, but candidates can earn a supplementary grading of 'distinction' or 'merit'.

The importance of G.C.E. lies in the fact that success in it at some level is accepted as a minimum qualification for entry to universities, colleges and professional courses. For colleges of education, which train teachers, the minimum entry requirement is five O levels, though many entrants have more and A levels as well. In general, the universities' minimum entry requirements are five or six O levels and two A levels. Again, satisfying these minimum requirements does not guarantee a place. Competition means that individual universities have plenty of people with more than the minimum requirements to choose from, so they, and particular faculties or departments, may insist on specific grades in certain subjects as a requirement for entry. They may also take into account the supplementary gradings mentioned earlier.

Unlike C.S.E., G.C.E. examining boards were formed by the universities, and the universities still run six of the eight boards, though teachers advise on syllabuses and are employed on marking the scripts. Overall responsibility for the examination, as with C.S.E., lies with the Schools Council.

EXAMINATIONS IN TECHNICAL COLLEGES

Both C.S.E. and G.C.E. are taken mainly by pupils in schools, but they are not the only examinations open to adolescents. There are an enormous number of courses in technical colleges and colleges of further education which lead to examinations. Many of these courses can be taken part-time and in the evenings. The largest of the examining bodies in technical education is the City and Guilds of London Institute. It holds examinations, prepares syllabuses and awards qualifications for craftsmen, technicians and others. Very many of these are for young workers in apprenticeships in engineering, building and the like. Most of them have left school at fifteen or sixteen and are seeking to become skilled manual workers. For apprentices and others, the 'City and Guilds' is as familiar a landmark as G.C.E. is to school pupils.

A boy showing ability on a craft apprenticeship course may be urged by the college, or by his firm, to transfer to another course leading to the Ordinary National Certificate (O.N.C.). These certificates, together with those at the higher level (H.N.C.), are awarded by joint committees of the Department of Education and Science and the appropriate professional institution (the Institution of Electrical Engineers, for example) on the basis of course work and examinations of the colleges assessed by people appointed by the joint committees. (In a way they foreshadowed the principle underlying C.S.E. mode 3.) These certificate courses are part-time ones. There are comparable courses, which are full-time, leading to

diplomas – O.N.D. and H.N.D. The standard reached at
O.N.C. and D. is thought to be comparable with that of
G.C.E. A level, and it is increasingly accepted as comparable
with A level for entry to university and other degree courses.
My own view is that the standard in national certificate and
diploma courses is higher than that required at A level. The
standard of H.N.C. and D. is held to be comparable with that
of a university pass degree, though on a narrower front. One
ought to say at once that there is nothing very objective about
any of these standards. There is no measure of the quality of
training offered – and the value of the higher certificates and
diplomas depends not so much on any judgement about their
intrinsic worth as on the fact that the professional institutions
seem determined to restrict the part-time route to professional
qualifications.

On the other hand, the technical college sector does have
an avowedly degree-level qualification – that is the degrees of
the Council for National Academic Awards. The Council
awards degrees to those who are successful in courses and
examinations of polytechnics and other technical colleges
which the Council has assessed and moderated. What this
means is that there is a route to the highest qualifications
open to those who have left school at fifteen or sixteen. A boy
can embark upon a craft apprenticeship, transfer to an O.N.C.
course and qualify himself for entry to a course leading to a
C.N.A.A. degree.

HOW TO HELP

There are two main ways in which parents can help when
their children are in for examinations. The first is a matter
of provision, the second a matter of attitude.

All that I shall say about the need to provide a place for
work applies with particular force if your child is taking an
examination. Whatever the school or college provides, there is
little doubt that he will want to work at home. It really can

make all the difference if the conditions for work are reasonable. This may mean putting a desk in a bedroom and providing some heat in the winter. It is not fair to expect people to study in the main living room with all the distraction which that implies.

Almost more important, however, is the attitude one adopts. Most examinations demand some sort of skill or knowledge – but what all examinations require is confidence. The attitude of the candidate makes a measurable difference to his performance, however well he is otherwise prepared. Anxiety, on the whole, is no help, and most children have quite enough of it of their own anyway. This means that if you yourself are anxious and tense you should do what you can to hide it. The more relaxed the general atmosphere you can maintain the more helpful on the whole you will be. This is less easy than it sounds. After all, you may feel that a very great deal depends on passing the examination. You may feel that failure would mean a waste of a great deal of time, effort and expense. Maybe, but it hardly helps to say so. One way to avoid getting too fraught is to realize that there are alternatives. Failure is seldom the end of everything. Anyone who has got to the point of sitting for one examination is capable of trying an alternative. For example, if a child makes a mess of O level at school it is possible to have another go at the local college of further education. One of the most potent causes of anxiety in exam-takers is the feeling that they are trapped. The realization of other possibilities relieves this feeling.

Nor need you regard the examination itself with any great awe. Many people make the mistake of believing that the result of an examination says something about the candidates as people. But most examinations are far too crude to measure very much. Most of them do not even measure anything significant about the course which leads to them. It often helps to distinguish very clearly between being educated and preparing for the exam. It is not too much to say that there comes a point in every course where the candidate has to stop worrying about education, or even knowing anything, and concentrate on the business of passing the examination. Parents can help by not regarding the process with too much reverence.

Not only does one's life not depend on passing a particular exam: it is probably a mistake to make anything else depend on it either. To say that success will attract the reward of a motor scooter or to say that further support for education must depend upon a certain level of success may soothe a parent's feelings of power and righteousness, but it will almost certainly be no help to the child. Bullying and bribery of this kind are no prettier in parents than in anyone else.

Try, too, to respect your child's own methods of work. Everybody prepares for examinations in slightly different ways. You may feel that you know best – and so you might, for yourself. But it is not sensible to try to insist on particular methods of swotting. For example, some children like to have background music on the radio. Try to avoid saying every day things like, 'I don't see how you can concentrate with that noise going on.' Similarly, some children like going to each other's houses and revising their work together. There is no need to assume, even less to assert, that they are just mucking about. Try not to keep asking how things are going. It is a silly question and will attract a silly answer.

You are in a dilemma, of course. You wish to help, and may not know how. You may find that your elaborately contrived relaxation will be flung in your face as evincing a lack of interest. If you try to help you are quite likely to be accused of nagging. Remember, though, that the situation is probably worse for the child than it is for you. Parents at least ought to be mature and secure enough to accept the occasional examination tantrum. Examination times are not pleasant, but one's whole object should be to avoid making them positively worse.

Adolescence

Right at the beginning of this chapter I said that secondary education was, in essence, the education of the adolescent. This means that on top of the familiar demands which children make in their progress through school, you have to accept the fact that the children themselves are changing before your very eyes. There are plenty of books on adolescence and how to cope with it. The reason for mentioning it specifically here is that it tends to pervade and complicate all the aspects of secondary education from relations with teachers and choice of subjects to performance in examinations and attitude to leaving school.

Perhaps it is worth reminding ourselves of what actually happens to young people at adolescence. In the first place they grow faster than they did when younger – the 'adolescent spurt'. From about four onwards your children have been growing at a fairly regular rate, that is by about the same amount each year. But at adolescence they suddenly shoot up, growing half as fast again as they did in the years before. The spurt takes place in different parts of the body at different times. The leg length reaches its peak first, followed by the breadth of the body then by the length of the trunk. This skeletal spurt is followed by the muscles. The heart, like other muscles, grows more rapidly. The strength of muscles increases sharply as does the capacity of the lungs.

Some parents worry about these rapid changes and talk about children 'outgrowing their strength'. There is no scientific basis for this idea: a boy's strength increases rapidly throughout adolescence even though its fastest growth follows that of height. So for a short time a boy may not have the strength of the young adult he outwardly resembles – but he is much stronger than he himself was earlier. Changes occur not only in the size of boys and girls, but in their shape: after adolescence boys have the wider shoulders of men, girls the broader hips of women. Nor are the changes confined to size and shape. There are the familiar changes related to sexual development. In boys, it is the testicles whose growth quickens first, followed (alongside the height spurt) by pubic hair, the beginnings of a beard and hair under the arms. The growth of the penis also occurs alongside the height spurt and the voice breaks a little afterwards. For girls, the beginnings of growth of the breast are the normal first signs of puberty. Menarche, or the first menstrual period, nearly always occurs after the peak of the height spurt. The full reproductive function is attained perhaps a year or eighteen months later.

We have seen in Chapter 1 how this development differs both between boys and girls and between individual children of the same sex. And we have also seen how it is followed by both intellectual and emotional development. For example, most students of child development now accept that the capacity to think formally and logically comes with adolescence and depends on the maturing of the brain and nervous system. Fairly clearly the development of adult emotions can be seen to depend upon physical changes.

All this is a time of intense upheaval to individual boys and girls. It is a time of change, doubt, uncertainty and excitement. We are all familiar with the physical and social clumsiness of adolescents. It is almost as if they are learning all over again how to use their bodies efficiently, as if they are 'trying on' unfamiliar attitudes and characters. They may at the same time hanker for both the security of childhood and the responsibility of maturity. Their demands to be treated like an adult may coincide with their most childish behaviour. The physical changes they are undergoing may make them personally unprepossessing. They may become slovenly and self-concerned at the same time. The contrasts can be very startling. Adolescents can be awkward in striving after elegance, demanding while claiming independence, alternately mature and childish.

All this can make adolescents very difficult to live with. The trouble is that parents have had something like a decade in which their children have been behaving fairly predictably as children. Suddenly they change. It is often very hard for parents to change their own attitudes and methods. What is especially galling is the realization that there is in the house someone who is no longer a child, a mere dependent, but recognizably an adult – and *young*. So a parent's reaction may itself be complicated by envy.

Probably few families get through children's adolescence entirely unscathed. Perhaps the parents who cope most successfully are those whose attitudes to children while they were children have made it possible to accept the changes with good grace. For example, if you have always regarded your children as people in their own right, who make their own decisions and deserve consideration; if you have seen it as your job to help them towards independence; if you yourself have had a life and interests of your own apart from the rearing of children, you will almost certainly find the demands of adolescence less worrying. If, on the other hand, you have too many preconceptions about what your children 'ought' to be like; if you have made a heavy investment in them, emotional or financial; if you have been wrapped up in their progress, you may find the adolescent years peculiarly painful. It is a time to remember what I hope has been the chief lesson of this book, that in moments of crisis the best thing to do is relax if you can. Try not to make absurd demands. Try not to have too many principles on which you make firm stands. Above all, do not embark upon battles that you cannot win.

This is all very well in general, but how does it work out in terms of school? Let us take the question of choice. In the past, when choices have had to be made, the child was visibly dependent upon the advice of parents and teachers. Although he himself may have had a preference, he was probably reasonably ready to defer to adult opinion. Choices have in-

creasingly to be made as children get older, involving different subjects, different examinations, different careers. Many
parents try to act in the old ways, assuming that what they
say goes and will continue to go. The trouble is that the
child may no longer be ready to accept this assumption. To
make matters worse the parents' experience and knowledge
may be visibly inadequate. The relationship is quite changed.
In this situation it is no use at all beginning a battle lasting
several months which comes to dominate the whole of family
life – yet many parents do it. It is reasonable for parents to
put their point of view as strongly as they believe necessary –
but not too often. If the advice is accepted, well and good.
If it is not, and you fear disaster, the thing to do is to discover
quietly some of the alternatives mentioned earlier in this
chapter if disaster ensues. You will rarely fend it off by being
aggressive: you may even invite what you seek to avoid.

Or take the demands of school work. It is clear that
examinations mean consistent study and that consistent study
is best done against a background of regular meals and
adequate sleep. It is reasonable to try to explain this, even to
appear concerned, but many parents go much further than
this, and I suspect that they use the demands of examinations
as a rationalization for their desire to stop young people
having a good time.

I have already discussed the question of whether or not a
child should stay at school after the compulsory age. Parents
who insist on this very often have some picture of what they
expect their children to be: they may even feel it is essential
for the children to develop like themselves. But adolescence
above all is no time for presuppositions. There is less need
for insistence here than for discussion with pupils and teachers
alike about all the possibilities and about all the child's
capacities.

In that adolescence is a time of asserting adult individuality,
a certain amount of rebellion is inevitable. Nor is it any bad
thing that young people have parents to rebel against. What

the young do not realize is that for the moment (and until they themselves are parents) they are bound to win. If they did realize it they might be nicer. But parents can realize it and act more gracefully. Above all, they can seek to avoid importing into the questions and decisions about schooling the crises which arise not from school itself but from the changing relationships between one generation and the next. If your son is determined on a course of action you think unwise, it is more important to assure yourself that other options remain open to him and that he knows what they are than that you assert yourself and your own ambitions and values.

9 Home Background

Each child reacts to school in his own individual way. Each needs something slightly different from his parents by way of support at home. Parents with more than one child at school scarcely need to be told this. But it often helps parents of only one child or whose first child has just started school to know that other children are just as quirky though in different ways. For example, one child may get rather tired by the end of the school day. He may keep his self-control until he gets home, and then become thoroughly cantankerous. Another child (particularly a first child) may find school very stimulating: he enjoys the freedom and anonymity which he gets from being in a large group. Then he has to adjust to being on his own at home, bearing a great load of parental love, concern, interruption and nagging. He too acts up. What he needs, probably, is a little healthy neglect and something to get on with. (Many fathers need a stiff drink to get over the transition from work to home: children need a bit of help sometimes too.)

To take another example, some children enjoy talking about their school: they constantly recount stories about it and bring home paintings, models, samples of writing and so on. They sing school songs and hymns. All this helps parents to feel involved in what their children are doing. But others treasure the school as a private world where parents never intrude. They never bring work home, are disappointed if parents seem to know their school songs and, when asked to do anything resembling school work (like reading or writing), balk at it stubbornly. Parents of such children may often feel, with Lady Bracknell, that 'in England at any rate education produces no effect whatsoever'. It is clear that the detailed reaction of parents must be very different with different children. Take your cue from the child: if he talks, listen; if not, respect his privacy. But, if the normally silent child happens one day to mention school, try not to be engaged in something so 'important' that you have to brush him aside. You can of course find out more about what is actually going on in school from teachers as occasion arises (see Chapter 10).

All this means that a chapter on the kind of home background that is helpful to children must be extremely general; in reading it, you should bear in mind the specific suggestions made in earlier chapters. Nor is this a book about child-rearing, so this is not the place to discuss at length the need for love and security, the place of discipline or the choice of friends. But all the things which baby and child books recommend will give children at school the basic general support they need: consistent treatment, regular habits, sensible priorities and, above all, facilities for doing what they want, whether this is being quiet or noisy as the mood takes them. Parents need these things too and if they can arrange it for themselves and their children, and to treat their children as individuals, they will find that it helps at school and that the children will be nicer to live with, too.

The bulk of this chapter concerns what you can provide in the way of space, time and materials, and my hope is that it takes account of the practical circumstances of most families. Towards the end of the chapter I turn to specific things that parents often ask about, like toys, homework, television and so on.

Space

One of the first things that children need in their home background is space. This is easy to say, but often difficult to provide in this tiny overcrowded island, with its consistent tendency to damp and cold. Some families find it hard to offer the space which growing children need for physical games and exercise. Others may be isolated, so that the companionship of other children takes some arranging. Yet others are overcrowded: their difficulty is in finding privacy for parents and children. Few families are so well off that they can provide everything or so badly off that they can provide nothing. What I mean to try and do in this section is to show how parents can make the most of normal or even unprepossessing circumstances to provide for what their children most require. The drawings are by Janet Turner, who herself has two children. I asked her for her suggestions of what could be done to make space available for children even in very modest houses. You will see that her drawings are concerned with using small bay windows, spaces in the roof and under the stair, box-rooms and recesses formed by chimney breasts. Of course, this section is not meant to be exhaustive: many parents will find, I hope, that they themselves have more ideas than I am offering here, and better ones at that. Perhaps the best thing a book like this can do is to suggest that few people are entirely at the mercy of circumstances, that there is a lot they can do and that their own ideas are worth pursuing.

There is one more general point to be made. Children may need both the facilities and the opportunities to pursue their own interests, but more important than either of these is the attitude of the parents. I know of families living in very straitened conditions whose children nevertheless feel encouraged to do a great deal at home and who feel that what they do is valued. On the other hand, there are children in desirable residences who may always feel that there are more important things than their activities going on around them and who are constantly giving way to the priorities of others. If a child is constantly being tidied up and his productions dropped in the dustbin, he will quickly come to feel that little importance is attached to what he does, and he will

Many small houses do not have room for a separate study or workroom. A simple solution is to build shelves in a recess or alcove incorporating a pull-out extension for working at.

feel this however splendid his room and however frequently he is bought expensive toys and equipment. Being a good parent is not a matter of wealth: it is a matter of attitude.

Accommodation

If you take an average family and have a look at their house it is hard to believe that the one was designed for the other. A father, a mother and two children may typically find themselves in Britain with a house of two floors, the bottom consisting of what the house agents call reception rooms, kitchen and hall and the upper of two bedrooms, a bathroom and a dwarf room. The latter is there not because anybody wants it but because of using the space over the hall. What should our family do with the accommodation available?

In the first place they can find ways of using all of it. This may sound obvious but in fact many British families use only a small part of these small houses. It is entirely normal for there to be only one room downstairs which is sufficiently warm and well lit for people to want to sit in. The rest of the house remains unheated, and thus, for most of the year, unusable. The end of each day means a trek from the warmth of the living room to the frigidities of the bedrooms upstairs. For some people the second downstairs room is equally isolated by being kept as a 'best' room which is used only when visitors appear. All this adds up to an astonishing waste. You are, after all, paying for the whole house (either in rent or through a mortgage) or have actually paid for it. You are not paying for a couple of rooms which are in constant use. with the rest thrown in free. Yet it would certainly transform the lives of many families if they acted upon this simple fact. Of course, a lot of people believe that the expense of arranging to heat the other rooms would be too great, and

Loft conversion gives more space in the normal semi-detached house. This one has a work bench–homework top, bed and good spot lighting as this room would have poor daylight. The single pedestal desk is in whitewood with three plastic drawers mounted under the work top.

Under stairs. When no rooms are available this tiny area can be used if fitted out with shelves and a desk top or deep shelf for working and good lighting.

it is true that if you heat your whole house the fuel bills go up. But this is not the only consideration. The calculation you have to do first is to see how much you are paying for the basic accommodation and then discover how much extra you have to pay in order to be able to use all of it. To take an example, if you are paying £15 per week for your house, are using only two rooms and it would cost an extra £1 to make the whole house usable, it would certainly be common sense to try to manage it somehow. As every small businessman knows, if you leave plant idle you are losing money.

It is important to remember that this is not a luxury. In these over-crowded days, people are making the realization very clearly that individual human beings have a basic need for a certain amount of space and privacy. When we are denied this, as one author dramatically put it, we behave like animals in captivity. A lot of the difficulties of families with growing children arise directly out of the fact that they are trying to live with too little space and too much community. In these circumstances it is scarcely surprising that the family should anaesthetize itself with the television. It should not need saying that it is not only children who need somewhere which they can call their own, somewhere where their things are undisturbed and somewhere where they can get on with their own business without disturbing others. Adults need this too.

Let us assume then that a family is able to use its three-bedroomed house because it has managed to have the rooms heated by one of the enormously varied methods now available. Many people still feel that they want a separate dining room – this keeps the business of eating relatively isolated –

Any 7½-by-10-foot wall in any room. Whitewood units with plastic work top and shelving; electrified track for record player and localized spotlight.

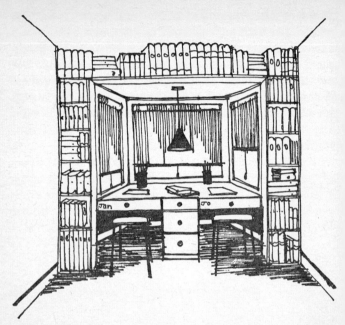

Bay-window unit in semi-detached or villa-type house, utilizing even the surround to the bay area for books, provides an adequate work-study area for two children. The lighting point is often in this position in this type of house.

and many find that this room can also accommodate the television. But there is still the second room downstairs – often the largest and most attractive room in the house. Traditionally this is rather a special room, to be used only on special occasions, and in a sense every family needs such a room which they can keep nice and entertain their visitors; but it would be a great pity if this room were used by everyone except the family, when it could well be a place for getting a bit of peace and quiet, or for general family chat. It is no bad thing if there is at least one room in every house where children are normally excluded. This immediately becomes possible if the rest of the house is available to them. It is in the nature of children to make a mess. Children involve spilt glue, leaking felt pens, the clueless use of scissors, jagged edges of old toys and a good deal of sheer dirt. There are some people who find all this lovable, or at worst a matter of small importance, but there really is no reason why this invasion of childish squalor should cover the whole house.

Room over the hall, often 6½ by 8½ feet. By lifting the bed the area underneath can be used for storage and clothes hanging. Whitewood or single filing-cabinet with shelving to ceiling height. The window is masked with a holland blind, most suitable in tiny rooms to give uncluttered appearance.

It is entirely reasonable for parents to insist that one particular room – call it the drawing room, lounge or what you
will – shall be free of it. The children also benefit from this
arrangement, if indirectly. The urge to keep them un-
naturally tidy elsewhere will be that much less if parents have
at any rate one haven of their own. If the dining room is a

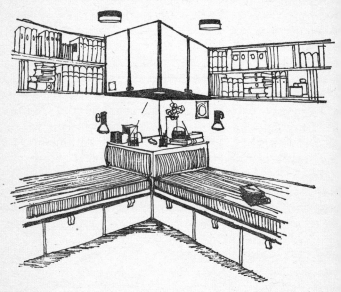

*Bedroom for two with storage under mattresses and corner cup-
boards suitable for teenage children, with good reading-light and
adequate book storage.*

family room then perhaps the other downstairs room should
be the parents' room. Of course, the idyll of this notion can
be quite as easily disrupted by a father or a mother as by
any children, but it is not the business of this book to contribute to what might be a matrimonial disagreement.

This leaves us with the bedrooms, and this is the point
where it seems to me there is some scope for increasing the

amount of accommodation available. My own view is that one should try to arrange that a child's bedroom is, as it were, 'his' room, that what goes on in it should be his business and that he should be relatively free from outside interference. Of course, it may not be possible for each child to have a complete room. In our typical three-bedroomed house, there is the immediate difficulty that if each of two children has a room one will have a large room and the other a boxroom. Allocation is often decided on the basis of age. This can lead to resentment on the part of the younger child and you might consider whether they could be enticed to swap round on occasion. If our typical family has three children then two of them are going to have to share a bedroom and will have at best areas or corners of their own. In any event, few families are going to be so well off for space that they can afford to waste any, and all the suggestions which are any use are those which help you to get a quart into a pint pot.

There are, of course, some very simple principles. First is that there is more space in a room than most people think. A second is that you can put things on walls quite as well as on floors. Another is to make sure that if something takes up a lot of room it really is doing a worthwhile job. Let us see what this means in practice. In the first place, if rooms are very small indeed, don't go in for huge beds. Few children need a bed more than two feet six inches wide, and they can do with the extra space left in the room to play in. A divan is normally more use than a frame with knobs on. Normally, a bed wastes space that can be used for storage in drawers or boxes underneath it. Similarly, many people waste all the space above the bed too, but one can in fact cover walls with shelves and cupboards. Shelves can eliminate the need for such space-wasting objects as bedside tables. They are important too in keeping a child's things visibly available and they can make tidying up an actual pleasure. For example, if a collection of model motors is normally entirely set out on a shelf you will find that most people think them more fun, and equally (since putting things in order is itself pleasurable) putting them away can itself be a pleasure. Again, children do like to have places to display their treasures and the things that they make and collect – and they need somewhere for the books which all advisers on home and school relationships insist that a well-equipped home should have.

Shelves are not the only things that can go on walls. Certainly walls themselves should not be devoted chiefly to the display of attractive wallpaper. A child should be able to pin things up (there are plenty of suitable materials like corkboard which can be used for this purpose) and since most children like drawing on walls at some stage it is worth making this possible too, perhaps with a blackboard. Don't worry too much about keeping walls immaculate. It is true that wallpaper costs money, but you will find that children themselves will rectify their own disasters. For example, a scribble executed in a moment's experiment when young will get covered up later by a poster or map without your having to turn the place out or get the decorators in. If the mess on the wall irritates you, stop worrying. Remember your own sanctum in the front room downstairs and go and relax in that.

If you have cupboards and shelves on the walls, the other furniture essential in a child's room is a table and chair for writing or drawing at. These need not be very elaborate either. In fact, some parents find it possible to fix to the wall a piece of wood which folds out to form a desk top, leaving more space when it is not in use. The important thing is that it should not be too wobbly and that it should indeed do the job for which it is intended. The only piece of furniture which is almost impossible to accommodate in a very small room is a wardrobe. The width of the average coat hanger ensures that you can seldom get away with anything less than two foot square. This can be a very swollen item in a confined space. With young children the problem need not arise, since small clothes can be folded away in drawers and cupboards. Even later, when the problem becomes more acute, it is often possible to decide on a minimum number of garments which really need to be hung full-length and to put these all in one wardrobe which can be as conveniently housed as possible. It is often a good idea to use an awkward-shaped recess as a cupboard for this purpose. What all this amounts to in a child's room is a minimum amount of furniture with the maximum amount of storage space, leaving the floor free for play and other activities. One seemingly trivial decision can make a lot of difference in this too. Try to see that the floor covering, whatever it is, goes from wall to wall. This not only makes it very convenient to play on. It is also very much easier to tidy up and clean. It is far better to have the cheapest wall-to-wall covering than to have an expensive centre rug. It is a help too if the carpet is corded or made from some artificial fibre. It should not be a long-haired and moulting affair. When buying a carpet for the floor think of it in terms of plasticine and chewing gum.

Another thing you can do is to make it easy to tidy up. This is partly for the benefit of whoever cleans the room. However strict you are about children packing things away, there will be occasions when mother, or even father, has to do it. But ease of tidying is also for the benefit of the child. The inevitable job becomes that much less of a chore. The main positive advantage is that his possessions are more readily available when needed. We all know of children wandering about claiming that they are bored and have nothing to do when they actually have mounds of stuff, but in such a muddle that they cannot clearly see any of it. Apart from fairly narrow shelves for displaying collections or models and appropriate shelves for books, perhaps the most obvious need is for various sizes of boxes into which different groups of toys can be put. There may be a box or space for table games like snakes and ladders or ludo, a box for Lego, Meccano or other building systems, another for a model railway, little boxes for marbles, cigarette cards and the like. The list can be endless. My own ideal is to be able to have a set of receptacles ranged round the room so that one can sit in the middle of the floor and toss the surrounding rubbish directly into its place, and then close some doors upon it all. Needless to say, this ideal has not been achieved.

Of course, not every child can have a room of his own. Probably most children share. Many families do not have the three-bedroomed house of the example quoted earlier. But the principles remain the same. Try to give each child a place of his own, where his things can be. Try to make it possible for there to be somewhere where the children have priority. And remember that parents need a place where they have priority too.

Outdoors

It is a persistent English dream to have a house with a garden, and it certainly helps if children have a space in which they can play safely. Unfortunately, not all families with gardens let their children play in them. There is a real conflict of interest. Even if parents do not have a passion for roses or lawns, they are likely to want the garden to look nice. They may even want to sit in it on long summer evenings. Children seldom give a high priority to the look of the thing. Football is incompatible with billiard table lawns or delicate shrubs. You have to compromise. Again, it is best if different members of the family have definite areas they can call their own. If father must have marvellous roses, cannot he be persuaded to make a screen of them behind which the children can create confusion, concealed from the house and the al fresco tea parties? It is the *mess* that you have to accept. Many parents feel that all will be well if they give their children a patch of soil in which to grow things. Some children do get enthusiastic about such an idea for a day or two, but it will not be long before they want to dig a trench or arrange a flood. Some fathers romantically provide wood and other material, expecting the children to build an acceptable hideout. What actually happens is that the stuff gets scattered about and lies rotting in odd corners or blanching the end of the lawn. Children seldom fulfil our ideas of what they are likely to do. They get their fun in mysterious ways, and too much direction is no fun at all.

I am not sure, in the end, that a garden is not something of a lost cause, at any rate while children are young. It really does seem unreasonable, if one has space, for them to be constrained in the use of it. I would not recommend going to the lengths which my own parents managed – of handing over the garden entirely with the consequence that every child in the neighbourhood could be found in it – so that there was for several years a pit five feet deep with several trenches running off it within fifteen yards of the back door. But one should probably settle for a fairly rough lawn and some extremely hardy shrubs and other plants.

One of the difficulties about giving a garden to children is the neighbours. They may complain about the noise. They may become murderous on account of the number of balls that fly over the fence. Of course, it can be infuriating to be constantly bothered by children wanting to get their ball back, and it can be worse to have a particular treasured plant broken. If you have a fussy or unfriendly neighbour, there is not much you can do except minimize the nuisance as far as possible. There are games which can be played in the garden which do not involve footballs or tennis balls, and it might be possible to encourage an interest in those. The odd thing is that one can never tell in advance how neighbours are going to react. One of the most unreasonable neighbours I know of is a local inspector of schools.

Perhaps the most galling thing for parents with gardens is to find that, after they have been liberal-minded and generous in handing it over to their children, the children actually prefer to play in the street. Cheer up, this is almost certainly a 'phase'. If there is danger in the street, you will of course try to keep them out of it, but otherwise the thing to do is wait for the fashion to change.

For many children the street is the only resort. In many cities families live in high flats or back-to-back houses. In the suburbs, there are increasing numbers of 'developments' in which the houses have a tiny patch at the back, or a 'patio', with the compensation of a landscaped bit in the front. For people in these circumstances one can but urge the use of public parks and open spaces. On the other hand, a number of groups of parents have had some success in establishing playgrounds and play spaces nearby. The adventure playground movement has made acceptable, at any rate to the authorities, the sort of derelict haven which is attractive to children. The need for outdoor space is beginning to be recognized, so that an argument with a local authority may turn not so much on the need, but on the possibility of meeting it in a particular case. If you live in a council flat and there is no play space nearby, then get on to a local councillor, preferably with a group of other parents, and nag him until one is provided. If you live in one of these new experiments in communal living, then make sure there are people with children on the management committee so that there can be a proper balance of the claims of those who want the public space to be usable and those who want it to be largely ornamental.

Time

Most people can see the need for space indoors and out in bringing up children. Perhaps fewer parents understand the need to provide time. It is a fact of life that parents and children spend much of the day outside the home. It is also true that in the home itself there is much to be done. The school may make additional demands in the way of homework. But despite all these pressures it is important that the family should *meet*. This book takes for granted the overall need for strong and loving family relationships. But if you are to support your children at school, and create a helpful home background, you do need to get to know them. It is, for example, very difficult to solve problems by tackling them as swiftly as they arise. You will find that the problem is obstinate. And even in unproblematic circumstances parents often underestimate the time it takes for children to learn. You cannot expect children to chat about their doings at school to order or by appointment. This sort of communication can come only if it arises naturally, in a situation where the children are encouraged, in the normal course of events, to chat about what they are doing. Nor can you expect a child to have the confidence to mention a problem if you have not established a relationship in which this sort of discussion is normal.

There are two kinds of problem here. The first is one which is encountered mostly by mothers. Running a home is more than a full-time job, much of it not very enticing. There always seems to be something left to do. Somehow sitting and chatting, or even just watching children, smacks of idleness. Shouldn't one be washing up or thinking about the evening meal or turning out a cupboard? Mothers can so easily get distracted by day-to-day chores.

But in the last resort nothing in the business of running a home need take priority over listening to and talking to children. Of course, the children have to be fed, clothed, shopped for, cleaned up after, nursed and the rest of it. But it is not always efficiency in these things which makes a good home. We have seen in earlier chapters what an advantage it is to children to be confident and articulate. These qualities can be well fostered at home if a child can rely on a hearing.

Fathers have a different problem. At work they become used to a certain kind of communication, a pace of operation, a set of impersonal relationships. This is quite unlike what happens at home, and many fathers find it very difficult to adapt. They may find the conversation of children pointless and boring. Secure in a particular job or process, they may forget that children have to learn to do things – quite ordinary things. They may unconsciously feel that one ought to have to say things only once to get results. The antidote to all this is time spent with children.

The fact is that for both mothers and fathers with other important things to think about, children can be an interruption and a distraction. And if they are, they are a burden. But if you concentrate on them, you will adapt to their pace, you will understand what they are saying and will see their problems if they have any. If they are on the periphery of your interest they will remain boring and baffling. If they come nearer the centre they will become interesting, even attractive. What this requires is *time*.

Order

Most books on child-rearing emphasize the importance to children of a regular routine, particularly about such things as meals and bedtime. The same considerations apply when one thinks of the home in terms of its being a background to school life. No child can get the most out of school if he is hungry or half asleep. On the other hand, a sense of order need not necessarily be the same thing as a timetable. The child who goes to bed without much complaint at *about* eight o'clock is in a more orderly atmosphere than one who goes at exactly eight o'clock after a very wearing wrangle. In other words, order is a matter of attitudes and atmosphere rather than rigid schemes. It also affects your attitude to school itself. Most parents understand that it is a good thing if home and school are not pulling against each other. Of course, there will be things which the school does which you disapprove of, but it helps if these are isolated instances: try not to set up a pair of warring worlds for the child which meet only to clash. It is perhaps worth saying a little more both about this aspect of home and school relationships and about the morning and bedtime routine.

MORNINGS AND EVENINGS

Mornings can be particularly difficult. Many parents get out of the habit of having breakfast and thus find it hard to persuade their children to have it. Persevere. Eat some yourself if you have to. It can make all the difference later in the morning. Indeed, the objection to stopping the free third of a pint of milk in junior and secondary schools was because of its importance in mid-morning when many children were flagging for want of food. If children do not seem keen on the breakfast provided, try a change of menu, although first thing in the morning is not the best time for culinary inventiveness. If the cut-outs on one cereal packet pall, try the models in another.

And it really is better if everybody can be got off in the mornings without a snarling rush. It is sad that the only weekday contact many fathers have with their children is roaring at them over the buzz of the electric razor. There must be very few families indeed who live up to those sparkling breakfast advertisements, but many parents may be interested to realize that many schools have come to regard the comparative lull of the initial assembly or act of worship as a way of helping the children to settle down, because half of them arrive at school in a virtual state of shock or derangement from the dawn chaos.

One way of preserving a certain amount of calm is seeing that the children have their school things ready when they wake up. This means having clothes laid out the night before. This may seem a bore in the evening when all you want to do is to put your feet up, but it pays dividends. Similarly if there are satchels full of books or bags of football kit, they too could be made ready. Another help is to eliminate all but essentials. Cleaned teeth, breakfast, a certain amount of clothing and necessary books and equipment are essential. It is not vitally important that every hair should be in place, every tie straight, every button fixed. Above all, allow enough time. There are some happy people who are at their sparkling best at eight o'clock, and there are others for whom waking up has something of the quality of a resurrection. If you are among the latter it helps to begin the process in time. I have discovered that it invariably takes three children half an hour longer to get ready for anything than it rationally should.

The quality of the morning after depends very often on the night before. Of course, not all children require the same amount of sleep. (We all know horror stories of children who wake up consistently for two or three hours in the middle of the night.) Equally there is no one ideal time for every child to be in bed. But it is not unreasonable for primary school children to be asleep by about nine o'clock. Like the rest of us, children sometimes need time to unwind, so it may help if they are reading or playing quietly on their own in bed for some time before they need to go to sleep. A warm bath may often help to relax them. If you have more than one child and you find that they keep each other awake by generally rioting about, you may find it wise to send them up to bed one at a time. It need not always be the youngest who goes first. And there is no need to feel guilty at all about sending them to bed in order to get them out of the way. Parents are people too and have their own lives to lead. It is entirely reasonable that you should be able to get on with your own affairs for most of the evening. But remember that this need not mean that you insist in too much detail on what the children actually do. You don't have to assert that they go to bed and sleep as soon as you say so: that is the way to begin a long battle. If you have two or more children you may in fact hear a certain amount of careering and thumping. Never mind.

As I said earlier, however, it is not the timetable itself which is important. What is required is that from the child's point of view parents are reliable. This means minimizing the occasions on which you act on a whim. It means that they come to be confident of your reactions, that you are relatively predictable. Naturally, children enjoy surprises, but the essence of a surprise is that it comes in the middle of the expected. It is unfair to children if they live in a world in which there is not very much rhyme or reason in what happens to them.

When in Rome . . .

Most children will want to conform to what goes on at school, inside the classroom and out. This is entirely natural, and you should try to help them to do so. For example, if the school has a uniform, most children will want to wear it. Some parents resent the demands which schools make about uniforms and may consider them dictatorial and absurd. A school may try to insist on shirts of a particular shade of blue obtainable only from a local supplier when shirts at half price are available from well-known chain stores, whose colour is barely distinguishable. Some head teachers *are* unreasonable. But don't have an argument for argument's sake. In the case I have just mentioned there are almost certain to be enough parents using the chain store for the argument to be settled before it begins. In other cases it is probably best to do what the school asks, even though it may be a bit daft.

There is of course the question of expense. A lot of parents can simply not afford to meet a series of eccentric rules. Different colours for different houses may mean that sports and other clothing cannot be handed down from one child to another. People who are in real difficulty here can often get help (see Chapter 11), and if you feel that you have need of a grant for school uniforms, do not hesitate to apply for one. You can get all the information about this from the school itself.

Children will also like to be able to meet small requests that the school makes for help with costumes for a play, for jumble for a jumble sale, with collections for under-developed countries and so on. Here again the main thing is that the child should be able to join in – you don't have to feel embarrassed if you cannot afford to do much. The thing is to do something. Very often schools put a limit on the kind of help they want or on the sums they expect to collect from individuals, and this can save a lot of embarrassment. Even if they don't, decide for yourself what it is you want to afford and stick to it. If you did but know, there are almost certainly richer parents than you giving less.

The problem of expense can also be acute when the school goes on organized visits in Britain or abroad. For some of these visits the basic cost may be quite low, but you may feel that the child ought to have the normal amount of spending money. For foreign visits, of course, the basic cost may be high. Here again, however, very many schools have funds which they set aside to help individual children. It is far better to accept any help which is available so that your child can join the trip than to prevent his going because you yourself cannot afford it. If you feel shy about it, you can be sure that the whole thing can reasonably be fixed up between yourself and the head teacher. In many schools, the staff who go on the visits do not know which of the children have been helped in this way. Increasingly, however, these foreign trips are arranged on an exchange basis: that is, children from a French school come to England to be put up by children of a school here – and then the roles are reversed in France. Again, a lot of parents become unnecessarily worried about this and fear that their homes or level of entertainment may not be sufficiently impressive. If you are already badly overcrowded at home, of course there is not much point in adding to it, even briefly. The child's school itself will be able to tell you whether your basic accommodation is enough. But again it is important to remember that these exchange trips are relatively cheap and people who go on them accept the possibility that they may be fairly modestly accommodated. Indeed, differences in home background are all part of the experience. You may feel that your guest will be comparing what you provide unfavourably with the experience of his friends, but in the end the impression that he takes away with him will be of how pleasant, friendly and cheerful your family was, and not the size of your living room or the comfort of your beds. And don't hesitate to take advantage of the fact that these exchanges are arranged between schools in the first place and not between individuals. In other words, you might well offer to put up a foreign student for a fortnight without your own child going away in exchange that year. Or you may find it possible for your child to go on an exchange, even though you have not been able to put up a foreign pupil yourself. The point to remember is that these visits are organized to help young people to meet their contemporaries abroad, not to be a burden all round.

Normally, however, conforming with what the school does and requires will be a matter less of these annual events than of small day-to-day decisions. Here, what a child gets out of school can depend to a large extent on your attitude to it. Children like to feel that what they are doing is right and acceptable, and this means that they are happier if they know that you support what the school is doing and what they are doing at school. You may find yourself disapproving of the methods, or the attitudes of individual teachers or of the school itself, and of course if the occasion arises there is no reason why you should not say so. But some parents find themselves carrying on a kind of critical running commentary on what the school is doing and once in this sort of mood it is all too easy to find continuous fault. As I have suggested, there is no need to suspend your critical faculties altogether, but if you are seriously dissatisfied you ought to see about moving your child. If you don't or can't do this, then make the best of a bad job. No school is wholly bad – indeed, most schools in Britain are really quite good – so discover what it is you like about the place and concentrate on that. After all, you cannot change what the school does, certainly not by nagging its pupils, so try to see that your child feels that home and school are not working against each other.

A relatively easy way to show general support and solidarity is to turn up at the functions which the school organizes. A lot of parents feel that the chief purpose of going to the school play or sports is to see their own children act or jump. But this is taking far too narrow and self-centred a view. Of course, it is important to children to feel that their parents are interested in what they themselves do, and they will be torn between wanting you to turn up and doubting their own capacity to impress you. But in some ways it is important that you show support and interest in the school as much as in your own child, so it is quite a good idea to attend events the school arranges, even when your own child is not taking part. If there is a parents' association, go along to this too.

It may be that in the end most parents are prepared to go along with what the school requires. On the other hand, many try to draw the line against their children conforming to their contemporaries. You ought to go a bit carefully here. Forming groups and making group rules and extending friendships are all an essential part of growing up, which starts at the junior school stage and goes on right up to adolescence. A child has to learn to get on with his own contemporaries, to be responsible for his own behaviour in the group and explore the limits of the contribution he can make. You cannot stop it and you should not try. The point at which parents are tempted to do so is when their child picks up an accent or an expression which horrifies them. Try not to be too put out. Children quickly scent disapproval at home and school and they learn to adopt quite different kinds of behaviour: one for home, one for the classroom, one for the playground, and so on. (One day my own children were giggling with some friends over some rude rhymes they had picked up, and the friends' mother was becoming quite worried because she thought her children didn't know any. She was both shocked and reassured to hear her own eight-year-old make his own contribution which he had of course not dreamed of telling her.) It is entirely reasonable that you should require your children not to be constantly offending your friends and relations. This too is a part of growing up. So stop the child swearing in the drawing room if you must, but don't keep telling him he has disgusting friends or that the school is terrible. Ask yourself if you would like him to keep telling you what he thought of your friends. The ideal is to have enough self-confidence in your own views and attitudes to believe that they will in the end turn out to be more durable in your child's development than the passing influence of even the roughest chums – and to accept that people differ in their social customs. In any case the chief offences of slovenly speech and foul language are scarcely of very much consequence.

Some parents, of course, have a similar difficulty if their child goes to grammar school when they themselves had very little education. They may feel he is growing away from them and getting all sorts of fancy ideas, and it must be admitted that some schools actively increase the difficulties of these parents and their children. It is often harder for such parents to retain the confidence to let their children conform to school if they want to. This too is a phase. The children themselves will become human beings again sooner or later.

More serious is the problem of the child who does not conform and who may be either permanently rebellious or permanently friendless and left out of things. Most children have periods when they are at odds with the world around them, but some children have more permanent difficulties and these are discussed more fully in Chapter 11. With a temporary difficulty your help should be unobtrusive if possible. One of the first things is to see that you are not insisting on behaviour which is held in contempt by other children, and to avoid doing so. Have a word with the child's teacher too, to see whether you can discover any other reasons for the child's isolation. At the primary school stage you can invite other children home or to join in an outing. This may in itself give you a clue as to what is wrong, but try not to work too hard at it – you might do more harm than good. In all this what you need is the flexibility and tact to meet changing and perhaps even contradictory demands.

Toys

In earlier chapters I have spoken of the need to have things in the home which stimulate a child's thinking, imagination and creative abilities. This means having all kinds of materials available, like wood, paper, cardboard, cloth, old clothes and so on. Perhaps most parents accept this, but feel that children also ought to have toys. Really very large sums of money are spent on ingenious gadgets, often by people who can ill afford them. There is nothing wrong with buying children toys, even expensive ones if you can. Children like the novelty, and it is always fun to receive presents. On the other hand, the most sensible attitude to toys is usually shown by the children themselves. Let us take an occasion like Christmas morning or a birthday to see what this attitude is. We all know the unruly scene. The child sits surrounded by booty, ripping off one coloured wrapping after another. Some parents cynically believe that this is the best part of the process, and that the toys will never afford quite the same pleasure again. The child will also try out one or two of the individual items. He may take up one particular toy or book and concentrate happily on that for the rest of the morning, leaving all the others discarded. Another child may simply sit back sated and bewildered, not knowing what to do when faced with so many alternatives. And we are all familiar with the Christmas afternoon effect when children who have just been presented with pounds' worth of expensive presents mope around complaining that they have nothing to do. If you are lucky you can persuade them to go outside to play with an old motor-car tyre.

All of this suggests an attitude for parents. There really is no need for a continuous supply of expensive gadgets. It is quite easy to give a child too much, and it is equally easy to baffle with over-complication. Small toys bought as surprises are often more effective than large pieces for an occasion. Similarly, it helps if the toys are kept relatively tidy, so that they remain accessible. Many children are given expensive new toys when they already have an enormous quantity of unused stuff.

It is also a relatively safe rule not to be afraid of the simple. What one pays for in expensive toys is usually some ingenious mechanical contrivance. This has two disadvantages. In the first place it invariably goes wrong – or often arrives wrong in the box. In the second, a mechanical toy greatly limits what a child can do with it. The best toys are those which have a large number of functions, which children can use for all kinds of purpose. The much loved and cherished toys are precisely those which can change their 'character'. This is one reason why dolls (including the 'action man' version for boys) are so everlastingly popular.

So if you are going to spend money on toys, think in terms of sketchbooks, the enormous variety of coloured pencils and pens, the cheaper models to make, small push-about cars, balls of various kinds, dolls and so on. Pander to the instinct to collect, but let the things collected be modest and simple. If you must go for the big set-piece let it be something that a number of children can do together, like a board game, skittles and the like. Or of course you can always go for the grand mechanical contrivance which costs the earth and which holds the attention, if you are lucky, for an afternoon – but you should realize that you are buying it for obscure purposes of your own, not for the pleasure or benefit of children.

Books

You will be told so often by teachers and others that a home which contains books is a help to children at school, that it scarcely needs me to repeat the advice. It is more than a matter of just having the books, of course. It is a help if children come from a home which is used to reading, used to turning to books for information and entertainment. The important thing is to put children in the way of reading so that they not only want to learn but keep up their practice in it. One great advantage of books is that they come in very appropriately as presents. If someone asks what to get the child for Christmas or a birthday and you are stumped, why not suggest a book appropriate to his age? The situation in the children's book world is really pretty cheerful from the parents' point of view. There are an enormous number of very good books available and in spite of rising prices many of them are still not all that expensive. It is of course possible to pay the earth for some large and imposing tome – but there is no need to neglect the well-produced paperback at one-tenth of the price.

Even people for whom buying books would be something of a luxury need not do without them. Most towns have an excellent public library service, and it is a good thing to get the children in the habit of going to the library and choosing their own books. If you yourself are unfamiliar with the library, do not be put off. The children will almost certainly have been taught at school about using a library and may well be more at home there than you are.

Homework

Homework is a vexed question. Most people feel it should be unnecessary (as a formal exercise at any rate) in the primary school, though some of these schools set quite a formidable amount to those children expected to do well in the eleven plus. In these circumstances parents are torn between desiring a grammar school place and irritation at the method of getting it. Homework is much more common and accepted in secondary schools. Here, two or three hours a night might be quite commonly accepted. The work set may be simply practice in some formula learned in class – though with new methods this kind of thing is becoming less general. At its best homework can be an important help in training children to work on their own and take responsibility for their own education.

Where homework is set, it is best to help the child to get it over and done with. This need not be the moment he gets home: indeed, a break for play or television may be almost essential. But normally homework should be completed in good time. It should not become yet another excuse for sitting up late. On the other hand, the parents' role here is a relatively passive one. They should see to it that homework is possible, in the sense that the child has somewhere reasonably quiet and appropriate to do it in. You yourself don't have to police the exercise. Whether or not a piece of homework is done is the business of the teacher who set it, and parents normally make matters worse if they constantly enquire what has to be done and whether each piece has been completed. If one of the values of homework is that children themselves take responsibility for doing it, you only undermine its purpose by taking the responsibility yourself. Of course, children will do their homework in the bus or on their knees at break time, and this may not be ideal. It is, on the other hand, almost certainly better than having a homework timetable imposed by the parents upon the timetable of the school day.

Parents often wonder whether they should help with their children's homework. They are getting less keen on this as teaching methods change and school subjects expand. There is certainly no harm in answering a child's questions here and there, if you can. But you should certainly avoid actually doing the work. If a child seems continually flummoxed, have a word with the teacher. The temptation to ask for help will probably be less great if the child has somewhere to do the homework other than the family living room. He is likely to get down to it more quickly and accurately too. There are some children who can do good work while watching the television but most do better if they concentrate.

Television

A lot of parents are still uncertain about television. When it first appeared in the majority of homes some parents (particularly middle-class parents) thought it ought to be forbidden like cigarettes or rationed like sweets. There were and are those who worry that there is too much violence, sex, rudery and irreligion to let children have too long with the box. Some moralists believe there is simply 'too much' television. Most of the early fears can now be seen to have been exaggerated. As with most things, children take from television what they want and largely ignore the rest. In some ways it can be a help: children whose parents are inarticulate or who appear not to talk to them can pick up a decent vocabulary, and for most children television does enlarge their knowledge and experience. The point is that children will seldom turn to any but their favourite television programmes if they themselves have enough to do and be interested in. They will prefer reality to its substitutes. Young children would normally rather their parents read to them than watch a story read on television. Older children will prefer playing imaginative games to watching television. What they need is a chance to do this. Naturally, if parents have the television constantly on in a sitting room which is the only warm and comfortable room in the house, and if the children have nowhere of their own to retreat to, of course they will watch it. In this case the box is no worse than boredom: there can be something very debilitating about both.

There is normally not much point in forbidding the television. It should be quite clear that it doesn't get in the way of necessary things like homework or sleep and there is little sense in letting the nervous child watch programmes which give him nightmares (if only to ensure that parents get a night's sleep). If the child seems to be seriously disturbed by a television programme or needs it as an escape from life, he needs serious help (see Chapter 11). It is not enough in this case just to turn the thing off.

My own objection to television is that it gets in the way of contact with the family. There is nothing more dispiriting than to arrive home in the evening to find the children sitting in front of the set, from which they do not budge until bedtime. It is not just the powerful feeling of irrelevance that one objects to – it is important to make time to talk to children and to listen to them. It is a good thing, too, if children are encouraged to choose. There is not much to be gained from looking in continuously, but there is every reason for letting children decide which programmes they most want to watch and have the television on for those. Perhaps my attitude to television is the rather puritanical one that most people, and especially children, should have something better to do than watch it very much.

There is one thing that parents very often do which is very hard to defend and that is deciding suddenly, while children are watching something, that it is time they went to bed or did their homework and simply barging in and switching the thing off, perhaps in the middle of the programme. This is usually unnecessary: television programmes are normally shortwinded, and one loses nothing by waiting to the end. To do otherwise is not only very rude but it also helps to destroy the child's concentration. It almost always provokes a whine or a row which is entirely unnecessary.

10 Contacts with Teachers

Before discussing the kind of contact it is possible to have with teachers, it may be worth looking at the kind of people that teachers are. The students who go to colleges of education (where teachers are trained), like the students in full-time higher education as a whole, come predominantly from middle-class families. Few of their parents are manual workers, skilled or unskilled. Those who have such parents quickly adopt attitudes and aspirations which make them indistinguishable from the rest. Most teachers were successful in their primary schools, they got into the A stream, passed the eleven plus and went to grammar school. From grammar school they probably went to college at eighteen and, having got the teacher's certificate, returned to the schools as teachers. All this means that the background and education of teachers are quite different from those of most children, including most of the children they themselves are teaching. If you yourself are a middle-class parent, or aspire to be one, you will find that you share many of the teachers' attitudes and assumptions. If you are a manual worker you will find that the teachers' assumptions and attitudes are different from your own, different from your children's and frequently hard to understand. This places a great responsibility on both parents and teachers. Teachers, like the rest of us, get on best with those they understand, so middle-class parents often find that they fit naturally into the arrangements which schools make to contact them. Working-class parents, on the other hand, may find the school remote and be put off by well-meaning attempts to attract their interest.

It is also clear that lack of understanding pervades the class-room. There have been many studies here and abroad which show how teachers' expectations effect the performance of their pupils. And teachers' expectations are rooted in their own background and upbringing. This means that they can spot 'ability' in the middle-class children more easily than they can in the children of manual workers, and they are known consistently to do so.

You may also like to know something about the ways in which teachers are trained. The teachers in primary schools and secondary schools have normally been to a college of education and taken a teacher's certificate. Today this is awarded after a three-year course. The minimum requirement for entry to a college of education is five subjects at G.C.E. O level, but in practice few students going to the colleges have qualifications as low as this. About a third have the two A levels which is the minimum requirement for entry to univer-sities.

The course in a college of education has four main parts. First there is the student's own personal education, for which he takes one or two subjects and studies them to as high a level as he can (perhaps to something like the standard of a pass degree). The second part can be called the study of education. The student teachers are taught about children, how they grow and develop, how they think, feel and learn, and about the social context in which this takes place. This part of the course includes history, sociology, psychology and philosophy. The third part concerns the act of teaching itself: the students study teaching methods and the theoretical basis of teaching particular subjects and skills. And this leads naturally to the fourth part which is practical work in schools. Colleges differ in the amount of time they devote to teaching practice and the variety of schools in which it is done. But the students themselves regard practice as the most useful and necessary part of their preparation for teach-ing. Recently it has become possible for students to stay in college for a fourth year and take a degree called the B.Ed. (Bachelor of Education). This is based very largely upon the theoretical, particularly the academic, part of the course.

It is generally agreed that the new methods in education which are most widespread in the primary schools, but which are now reaching the secondary stage, have been welcomed and put into practice by teachers trained in the colleges. On the other hand, teachers themselves have four main criticisms which are commonly made against their training. The first is that the course is too theoretical and too little related to the classroom; second, that it is wrong for teachers to be trained in isolation from other students in universities and colleges; third, that the intellectual level of many of the courses is too low; and fourth, that a teacher's career is isolated from 'real life' by virtue of the fact that he goes from school to college and back to school again as a teacher without any significant experience of the outside world.

About a quarter of the teachers in schools (most of them in grammar schools) have had different training. They have been to university and taken a three- or four-year degree course. After this they may have had a year's training as a teacher. New teachers in primary schools must have had training – and it will be required for new secondary school teachers after 1974. The training resembles the college of education course, except that the student's own personal education is assumed to have been taken care of by the previous degree course. (The whole question of teacher training has been the subject of a report by the James Committee, published early in 1972.)

These, then, are the people who are teaching your children. The question is how does one get to see them? Apparently most parents are satisfied with the contacts they have with teachers, at least if their replies to surveys conducted for the Plowden Report are to believed. On the other hand, half the parents surveyed said that they would have liked to be told more about their children's progress at school and one in three of them thought the teachers should have asked them more about their children. One in ten was not satisfied with the arrangements for seeing the head or class teacher; slightly fewer felt it was not easy to see teachers whenever they wanted to; one in fourteen felt that teachers did not seem very pleased when they went to schools and a similar number thought teachers would prefer to keep parents out of school. So the general satisfaction is tempered by some fairly definite grumbles.

But whatever the general picture, individual schools differ enormously in the extent to which they welcome parents. Some are open and free, others formal and forbidding. Few offer the 'minimum programme' of relationships with parents which the Plowden Report recommended. So, parents may either find themselves swept into a whirl of school activity or kept very much at arm's length. More usually they will be invited on occasion to some function or meeting. This may satisfy most parents, because most of the time children go uneventfully through their school careers. It is when things are difficult or worrying that a parent may wish the school did more, and here the initiative to make contact may have to be taken by the parent.

The traditional method of letting parents know how their children are getting on is the school report. Reports can be quite helpful, especially if they reveal to parents things they did not know about a child, like an unsuspected gift for mathematics or a capacity for responsibility. They can also help to give an idea of how a child compares with his contemporaries. Parents need to know how a child is developing and be able to value his achievements for their own sake – but they also need to know whether these achievements are normal for a child of his age or not. This is why school reports are full of marks and placings, or at least grades. The trouble with these is that they have an air of precision which is quite misleading. The most they give is a general indication of progress, and often quite large changes in an order of merit are pure coincidence. Most children in any class are bunched around the middle grades: it is only if your child drops from third in the class to thirty-third. or has an equally spectacular rise, that you need raise an eyebrow.

Of course, reports are frequently a waste of time, written hurriedly in the end-of-term rush in conventional terms. They mean very little to parents and raise the suspicion that the teacher scarcely knows the child. Parents soon manage to put their own gloss on these: 'satisfactory' means 'I cannot remember the child', and 'could do better' stands for 'I have written satisfactory too often.' But even when they are carefully done, reports can mislead. Try not to be unduly discouraged or alienated by a sharp comment. The very form of the report – often a printed return with a receipt slip attached – may make it seem more like a rite than a help. For this reason, some primary schools have taken to sending short letters rather than reports, and these certainly seem more informal, personal and helpful. The Plowden Report gave some examples of what it considered good practice in the matter of reports. The first was a traditional report which, however, included a space for parents to comment (see page 189). The others were suggested forms of letters that might be sent from primary schools (see pages 190 and 191).

The thing to remember is that reports are meant to give you an idea of how your child is getting on: they are not a kind of judgement. You can quite reasonably be pleased if the report seems to be a 'good' one – but there is not much point in rounding on the child if it is not. Little purpose is served by demanding of a primary school child, or indeed any other, why his arithmetic is lagging or why he does not pay more attention. If the child knew why, he would probably do better. Look out for danger signals, by all means, but if you are worried have it out with the teacher rather than the child. Anxiety and irritation tend only to make matters worse.

There is one other value of school reports which parents

often overlook: it is that reports can tell you as much about the teachers as they do about the children. This value is enhanced when reports consist of books of separate sheets, individually written up by teachers who thus do not see what others have written. Even a single sheet, with a dozen pithy comments, can give you a shrewd idea which teachers are worth turning to for advice.

Form of Report Involving Parents

REPORT FOR SCHOOL YEAR ENDING 1966

CHILD Anthony Brown   CLASS 4Y

SUBJECT		EFFORT	ATTAINMENT	GENERAL REMARKS
Mathematics	Mechanical	C	C	Has made especially good progress in English and interest studies as a result of his wide reading. Often displays real artistic talent in his interest studies. His mathematics do not quite match with his other achievements. I feel sure he will do well in his secondary school.
	Practical	B	B	
English	Reading	A	A	
	Written	B	A	
Interest Studies		B	B	

Social attitude

   Tony is self-confident and has a good number of friends.
   He is a good organizer of games and handicraft projects.

A excellent   B very good   C average   D below average   E poor

   CLASS TEACHER ....   HEADMASTER ....

Please cut off and return to school

REMARKS – from PARENTS
(Please add any comments, information or concern which may be helpful)

We are very pleased that Anthony has improved in his work since we came to the open day at Easter. He still seems worried about his arithmetic and we would be glad to know how we can help him. I have tried but he says he does not do it like that.
Thank you for your help.

Suggested Form of Letter to Parents (1)

A letter which might be sent by an infants' head teacher to parents at the end of the first term.

Dear Mr and Mrs . . . . . .

We thought you would like to know how Tony has developed during his first term at school.

He made a confident start as he had been well prepared by you and his sister. I know you were disappointed that he was reluctant to come to school on some mornings later in the term, when his first enthusiasm had waned. This is not unusual, however, and may have been caused by his not being quite well at the time, some upset with one of his friends or by a very natural desire to stay at home sometimes! We think he would profit by a further period of attending in the mornings only as he does get tired in the afternoons. Perhaps you could call to see us about this.

He loves stories and books, especially about animals. Perhaps you or his father could spare time to read to him. I think you will find him beginning to pick out words to recognize. He can already read the names of most of the children in his class. He can count correctly up to five and is beginning to want to paint and write.

He is more independent in putting on his clothes etc., though he still needs a good deal of help in this.

He is a sensitive boy who is often thoughtful for other people.

Yours sincerely,

Suggested Form of Letter to Parents (2)

A letter which might be sent by the head teacher of a junior school to parents at the end of the first term.

Dear Mr and Mrs . . . . . .

We thought you might like to know how Diane is getting on in her first term in the junior school.

She began very timidly. She is small for her age and perhaps feared the larger children, but she is now a happy member of the group. She is greatly respected by the other children because she is so agile and fearless in physical activity and this has helped her to gain confidence.

Her reading is satisfactory, though slow. Could you spare time to take her to the Children's Library in — Street? She would be quite able to choose suitable books for herself and would improve her reading speed by reading a greater number of fairly easy books.

She is coming rather slowly to an understanding of numbers. We feel it is important that she should not be hurried in this, because that would add to her confusion. It would be helpful if you could entrust her with small sums of money for shopping and help her to count the change.

She does not like to take part in acting but is most ingenious in preparing costumes for other children. Her painting is really lovely. We hope you will find time to look in some morning next term to see the children at work.

Yours sincerely,

Most schools offer a number of occasions (perhaps half a dozen) in the year when parents can visit them and talk to teachers. These include sports days, carol services, harvest festivals, open days and the like. These are not always convenient: fathers in particular cannot manage day-time events, and even mothers with other children may find it difficult. Some schools arrange for the younger children to be looked after, others content themselves with saying how much they wish they could. In any case, these occasions when the school is formally on show are not suitable for a long talk. The teachers are likely to have things to organize and must share their time with all parents. If the problem cannot be cleared up quickly the best thing to do is fix a future, personal, meeting. But the public function is often a good place for a parent to make a first informal contact with a teacher, especially for parents who hesitate to go straight up to the school alone.

Parents are normally ready to be interested in the way the schools are organized, in the size of classes, streaming by ability, educational objectives and methods, the school library and so on. Some schools are ready to explain to parents some of their problems, like staffing or the allowance for books. This sort of information is often given by the head teachers at evening meetings for parents. Like reports, these vary a good deal in quality. Some heads can be inspiring. Others may simply hector their audience. Some, perhaps shrewdly, allow little time for questions. Others explain at length what parents should do to help the school without seeming to consider what the school might do to help parents. Occasionally one hears a head who can make clear the purpose and methods of the educational revolution that has overtaken the primary schools.

At open days and meetings parents can get a general idea of what the school is like. They may still want to talk to teachers about their own children. Many hesitate to do this, and many schools encourage their hesitations. Few arrange individual interviews when a child first goes to school, few have stated times when teachers are available for talks. Even the natural time for contact, when children are collected from school and teachers could be available in the playground or classroom, is often a well ordered exercise in disengagement.

On the other hand, even the most hostile schools are seldom as frightening as they seem. The notice on the door asking all visitors to report to the head teacher may be directed more against undesirable strays than parents. And it is hard to imagine a school directly refusing a request for an interview, though it may prove impossible in some to meet a child's class teacher. The thing to do is write or telephone and arrange an appointment. As with most things, contact with teachers requires practice. A parent going into a primary school for the first time may well be over-impressed. A head teacher's talk to parents is probably a well-repeated affair, the parents' reaction is likely to be naïve. In an interview a parent may be side-tracked and fail to put the point that worries him most. Experience helps. Parents soon put their own gloss on school reports. They know that speech days will mention the school's strengths and leave its failures unsung. They quickly detect, on an open day, if all the art has been contributed only by star pupils. They may come to guess quite shrewdly how far the progressive phrases of the head teacher are matched by practice in the school.

Parents need not be shy of asking questions. At open days it is not enough just to admire. Ask *why* the work was produced. Don't be afraid of the obvious question: 'But do they really learn to read (write or do arithmetic)?' If you do not understand some part of the headmaster's talk, ask about it. If it puzzles you, it will almost certainly have puzzled others. You are unlikely to be uniquely stupid, and the simple-minded question may be just one to reveal a good deal of pretension. And in interviews particularly, be sure you know what it is you want to know. Write it down if need be and refer to it in the interview. Taking notes is quite a good plan for timid parents. It gives them something to look at instead of the head, and it suggests that the parent is going to consider the interview after it is over, which is no bad discipline for the more blustery heads.

But, above all, remember the absent purpose of the whole exercise: the child. What needs to be done is what is best for him. You may wish to protest, to see that the teacher understands your point of view, to assert your parenthood, to vent some unconnected frustrations, to understand the meaning of modern education . . . whatever it is, it must be subsidiary to the task on which parent and teacher are engaged: the development of the child. A teacher or head teacher may talk naturally in terms of the school, what it does, how it is arranged, what its limitations are. The parent's interest is in the individual child, in how what the school does affects him. The purpose of their meeting is to see how the particular child can get the most from that particular school environment. If the school is seriously unsatisfactory, find another. No child enjoys having parents and school at loggerheads.

In a growing number of schools contact between parents and teachers is formalized in a parent–teacher association (P.T.A.). These naturally vary a good deal. Some meet infrequently, often for somewhat stilted 'social evenings': others are a powerhouse of ideas and activity for the school. Teachers often distrust P.T.A.s because of the myth that such associations virtually run schools in the United States (there is no evidence for this). Obviously those teachers who think that parents should be seen and not heard need no myth to support their attitude. Even so, parents need not despair if there is no P.T.A. at their child's school. There are other ways of fostering contact. Nor should they imagine that if contact is bad a P.T.A. will necessarily put it right. A good P.T.A. is normally the expression of close contacts, not the origin of them. Close cooperation takes time to create (often longer than the school life of any one child) so forming a P.T.A. is seldom the way to make contact on account of a particular child. It all depends on the head teacher. Those who favour P.T.A.s will normally suggest one themselves. Some may hang back because of opposition from their staff or a sizeable proportion of them. So if there is no P.T.A. and you and a number of other parents are interested in forming one, talk to the head. In general it is wise to suggest what the P.T.A. might do for the school, underemphasizing at first the good you think it will do the parents. P.T.A.s have certainly improved the physical amenities of many schools. They raise funds; build swimming pools, greenhouses, 'information centres' and museums; lay out gardens; run summer schools – as well as providing invaluable refreshments at school functions. They can also form an effective pressure group if the school seems to be left out of the local authority's building programme (religious school P.T.A.s are especially active here). There is no point in pressing these luxuries on unwilling teachers, but if the school would like a P.T.A. you can get advice from the National Federation of Parent Teacher Associations.

11 Problems

All children have difficulties. Parents are not perfect, and schools, being institutions (however child-centred), cannot be ideal for every child all the time. Most children manage to deal with their problems, given time and their parents' love, understanding, common sense and readiness to learn. It is not that difficulties disappear 'of their own accord'. It is that, given normal attention, most problems can be dealt with, and parents and children alike may look back at the period of the problem and wonder what all the fuss was about. Some problems may simply be superseded. That is, their importance diminishes as time goes on. There are very few things that parents worry about in children that they are still worrying about when the child is eighteen.

A child's difficulties may be of many kinds. He may have a physical handicap from birth, like deafness or partial sight. He may be crippled later by disease or accident. He may be a slow developer or have emotional troubles which prevent his learning. He may become fearful or aggressive. And a child with one difficulty may accumulate others. A physically handicapped child may become emotionally disturbed and thus backward at school. Another may have an emotional disturbance which has a physical symptom like asthma. In all this the reaction of parents can be decisive. A normal child with a temporary difficulty needs reassurance and understanding, not anxiety or a constant nagging at the problem. So it is a help if you can be relaxed. On the other hand, because most problems, even serious ones, are more tractable if treated early, you ought to be alert for the danger signals.

This advice may sound contradictory: I am arguing for a kind of calm vigilance. One way of achieving it is to realize that in most cases one is not alone. The most familiar example of help at hand is the family doctor. There is a great and familiar battery of childhood ailments to which all children tend to succumb. There are always minor accidents in the home. Most parents cope with all this in a perfectly reasonable manner. But most parents probably call the doctor for measles or whooping cough, not only to treat the disease but to make certain that it is not something worse. The doctor not only treats the patient: he also reassures the parent. Or to take another example, probably many women have worried at some time or another about pains in their chest and had fears that it may be cancer. The sensible thing to do is to go to the doctor, because if the condition is serious it is better to tackle it early. If, as is more likely, there is nothing wrong, it is a good thing to be told so and to stop worrying about it. In the same way, if you are worried about your child for some reason, the thing to do is to have him looked at professionally – if only to stop yourself worrying. There are an enormous number of experts and agencies which exist to help, and there is every reason for making use of them.

In dealing with the more common problems which arise at school this chapter will thus follow a fairly predictable pattern. It will suggest what parents can do when faced with the normal, relatively minor, difficulties that children may encounter; but when the problem proves intractable, or gets worse, I shall suggest the kind of professional help that parents ought to seek. The point at which parents seek it must always be a matter for their individual judgement.

One very common mistake some parents make is to treat a minor difficulty as if it were bound to get worse. They over-react and treat not the problem in front of them but the problem they feel it will become. For example, a child may on occasion steal something, at home perhaps. This frightens some parents, who believe that the child has embarked upon a life of crime. They therefore weigh in like Moses with all kinds of warnings and prohibitions. But it is very unlikely that the child is going to become a habitual thief, and he should not be treated as if he were. The scale of one's response should match that of the child's action – not that of one's worst fears.

Another difficulty that faces parents whose children have problems is that the problems tend to take up all one's attention. The important thing is to treat the difficulty, certainly – but then to go on behaving towards the child himself as if he were normal. This sense of normality is what is most important – yet parents may be overwhelmingly tempted to reject, pity or over-indulge him, to concentrate on the disability rather than the child himself, even to neglect other members of the family. Other parents may disturb themselves with feelings of guilt or wear themselves out in an effort to compensate in some way. All this is entirely natural but it is worth trying to avoid it if you can. Try to enlarge, rather than to minimize, the extent to which you behave normally.

In all this it is a great help if both parents are agreed on the approach to adopt and are equally happy with it. Often, however, one parent may be especially tense and worried or may be especially easygoing and careless. To some extent this is inevitable, but it helps if the difference of attitude and approach is not too marked. Preoccupied and relaxed fathers should try to be alert for the point at which they ought to offer a little sympathetic understanding and at least take seriously whatever is worrying their wives. Even unconcern can be more effective when it is seeking positively to minimize both worry and its cause. Derision is no use to anyone. Equally, a parent who is very worried should probably seek help. Worry has a useful function as an emotional spur to action, but too much of it can get in the way. But it is not the purpose of this book to pontificate on marital relationships.

One last general point. If your child has some special problem, the school is the place where you can naturally turn for help. Teachers can allay many anxieties and may be able to suggest remedies. They can help parents to discover the extent and seriousness of a problem. All the arguments for cooperation between parents and teachers have redoubled force when children are in special need. It is here, indeed, that home and school relationships come into their own. If you are used to chatting with teachers, and if your child is used to the fact that you do so, it will be so much easier to consult the school about a particular problem. It will be possible, indeed natural, to deal with a difficulty before it assumes any importance.

Different Standards

One of the things which children have to learn when they go to school is that different people have different standards of behaviour. What is required at school may well differ from what they have been used to at home – and their own friends may have a third set of standards to which they will want to conform. Usually children take these differences in their stride and adopt different modes of behaviour to suit the company they are in. Some parents get upset when their children bring home the habits learned elsewhere. They may feel, for example, that their infant children have picked up little at school but loud language and bad habits. In particular, of course, the children are asserting their independence – which is one of the things you send them to school for. In part they are trying it on: they want to see how far the newly discovered habits are acceptable at home.

There is no need to make too much of this sort of conflict. Parents have rights, and there is no reason why you should not insist on your own standards at home in a matter-of-fact way. If you don't like swearing, you can stop it. On the other hand, if you are easily shockable you merely tempt children into repetition: they do it for the drama. Equally, if you are constantly nagging and hectoring you can infuriate children into even worse behaviour. Nor is there much point in nagging teachers about children's playground language. They are almost certainly aware of it and are reacting in whatever way seems to them to be best.

This question of behaviour is a good example of the way some parents react, not to what is happening but to what they fear it may lead to. These parents associate bad language and rough behaviour with delinquency and react as if to protect their children from a rake's progress. Things are rarely as serious as this – and if they are, the bad language is the least of your worries.

The other side of this question is that teachers these days very frequently complain that parents do not sufficiently insist that what they say goes. They say that children come to school half expecting to be asked to do things over and over again. Just as parents often ask what the school is doing to develop decent behaviour, so the schools very often wonder whether parents have done anything at all in this direction in the pre-school years. If you have a mind to complain about pupils' conduct, it is a good idea to notice, at the week-end, how often you have to ask or tell your own children to do something.

There can often, of course, be a genuine conflict of attitude between home and school. You may be the sort of parent who believes in reasoning with children and is successful in doing so. The school, on the other hand, may accept corporal punishment and a particular teacher may be a bit handy with a slap or a plimsoll. Alternatively, you may be a stickler for discipline and feel that the school is impossibly lax. If this is the case, there comes a point where you have to decide whether you want the child to continue in that school or not. There is not much sense in having a running battle about it. Whatever the school is doing, you cannot make its effect any better by criticizing it in front of the children. Nor is there much to be gained by storming up to the school in defence of a child who has been smacked. The child will be delighted to be able to set parents and teachers at loggerheads, but the effect on his behaviour may be somewhat different from what you intend.

Sometimes a group of parents may come to believe that a particular teacher is being unnecessarily brutal. This is hard to substantiate, because children do very much exaggerate. After all, the children go home every day so the marks of serious physical punishment would be hard to conceal. If something like this seems to be occurring then the parents should have a word with the head of the school. It is best if the conversation can take place at some other time than in the shadow of a particular 'incident', but this may not always be possible. Try to remember (though it may be difficult) that your object is to make life pleasanter for the children, not simply more unpleasant for the teacher. Remember too that when the conversation is over the head has to go on running his school, the teacher to continue teaching and the children to continue in his class. If any change is to take place it is more likely to be successful if it comes on the initiative of the teacher concerned. It may even be that the teacher is aware of his own difficulties and would welcome help in solving them.

It may be, too, that you suspect that your own child simply does not get on well with a particular teacher. Again, if the matter is really serious you might speak to the head about getting the child transferred to another class. Often, however, the teacher is aware of this too and may welcome the chance of a chat. This sort of personal difficulty is not in any way unusual; indeed, it is not wholly avoidable. Clashes of personality are as normal as they are unpredictable. In your conversations with the teacher it may help if you show that you understand this, that you are not coming to accuse and that you can accept that your own child may not be everybody's cup of tea.

There remains the question of serious delinquency or the risk of forming destructive habits, like drug-taking. Encounters with the police and the courts are beyond the scope of this book, though its general principles still seem to me to apply. If your child is taken to court you may find your emotions violently involved: you may rush to his defence or reject him utterly. Either course is understandable, if unhelpful. The point is that since you are so much involved, seek expert and dispassionate help. If a child needs legal defence, see a solicitor and take his advice. He will manage things better than you can, in the unfamiliar world of the courts. If the child has actually been engaged in serious theft, or beating people up or pushing drugs, you cannot reasonably hope to 'win'. But you can expect that any mitigating circumstances are taken into account, and you can even help to see that his sentence is rational.

As for drugs, many parents are in a poor position to be much help here since they themselves smoke or drink alcohol, and you may be told by your children that soft drugs do less harm than either of these. But there is no ground for writing any drugs off as harmless, and you would be right to be concerned about them. As with so many problems, timing can be crucial, and many schools are in a position to help through knowing how to recognize quickly when a child has started taking drugs. Here again, you will need expert help, from the welfare and psychiatric services. The point where these problems are of concern in a book like this is in discussing what you should do if you find there is a worrying degree of delinquency or drug-taking associated with the school to which your children go, in which they may or may not be involved. You may feel that there is nothing for it but to remove the child. If you cannot, or do not wish to take this step, the keynote is cooperation. There will almost certainly be a number of parents who feel as you do. It may be as well to consult with them first. But do get in touch with the head and the staff pretty early on. You cannot operate independently of them, and should avoid giving the impression that you propose to try. Just as with your own personal problems, it is important to go to the school in a cooperative spirit, avoiding blame and accusation. The problem is one which you share, and the question is what help parents and teachers can offer each other in dealing with it. The specific steps you take, the degree to which you seek the help of the police or the probation service, will depend upon the precise circumstances and the personalities involved. You will quite certainly find that people differ enormously in the extent to which they regard various activities as serious.

The more serious the difficulty the more important is the cooperative approach. Let us take, for example, a situation in which serious violence occurs in a school, perhaps over a period. When this happens, the school may try to keep the knowledge of it to itself. There are good and bad reasons for this. A good reason is that publicity about violence increases the likelihood of it. A less good reason, however understandable, is the wish to preserve the school's reputation. The teachers will be concerned, too, to preserve their own reputations and self-respect. Whatever you do must take account of all this. The most constructive way is to approach the school and ask what parents can do to help. Make it clear that you regard the issue not in terms of failure in the school but as a problem which home and school can cooperate in solving. And in many ways violence is a problem in which parents can have a powerful influence. It is they who can create the climate of opinion in which the carrying of various kinds of weapons becomes less and less usual. At all events, it is not enough to leave it to teachers, to officialdom and to the police – especially if you are then loud in complaints and recriminations. It is the atmosphere of 'them and us' which most effectively breeds violence. The alternative is to get together with other parents, see the head and his staff quickly and decide between you what can be best done.

The Effects of Anxiety

Many children get anxious at one time or another, and most

of them are able to cope. Some children react by developing small compulsions. The least serious and most familiar of these is meticulously to avoid the gaps between paving stones. Mild compulsions like this are entirely normal. The time to get professional advice is if a compulsion, like excessive hand-washing, takes up a lot of a child's time. Some children may also develop nervous habits like blinking, clearing the throat or various head movements. These nervous movements are normally quick and regular and differ both from the normal squirmings of restlessness and from the irregular movements of chorea or St Vitus's dance. Children may bite or pick their nails, twist their hair (girls may chew it) or pull their ears. Nervous habits like this usually mean that a child is tense and under pressure. Maybe school is a little too much for him, or more likely parents are being too strict or demanding. Sometimes the tension can be induced by an exciting book or television programme. Whatever the cause, it is clearly no use nagging a child about a nervous habit: that will only make matters worse. The thing to do is to try to make things more agreeable. Most nervous habits simply go away in time.

One particularly noticeable difficulty which often distresses parents is stuttering. You should try, if possible, to reduce tension, but even when a child is more relaxed the habit of stuttering may persist. Here, the expert you want is a speech therapist, and the school can tell you about speech therapy clinics and how to get in touch with them.

Some stealing in young children is almost a nervous habit. Often the thing stolen is quite trivial, or something the child has plenty of anyway. In this kind of theft, the child is often unhappy or lonely. He may feel that his parents do not love him enough or that he is not popular at school – though he may be wrong in both instances. If you come across thieving of this kind, try to avoid coming down on the child like a ton of bricks, though the temptation may be strong. You will probably want to see that the child is not lying about the theft and you may want to insist on restitution. But the object is to make clear that stealing is not allowed, not to humiliate the child. And your response needs to be fairly nicely calculated so as to prevent a recurrence – not simply to add to the initial cause of the stealing. Minor dishonesty in children is entirely normal and there is no need to over-react. If a child persistently 'forgets' to bring you the change from dinner money, you might consider whether regular pocket money might not help, or whether you can't give him the chance to earn a little by doing odd jobs. Similarly, if a teacher complains of petty thieving, you will treat the matter seriously but again with a sense of proportion.

Sometimes a child's worries show themselves in reluctance to go to school or an unwillingness to eat breakfast. Many mothers worry about children going out on an empty stomach (and elsewhere I have asserted the importance of breakfast) but if the child will not eat in the morning, there is little point in trying to force him. It may make him sick. It is probably better to go to school on an empty stomach than to start the day tense and miserable. Left alone, the child will probably get hungrier at breakfast time.

Reluctance to go to school on occasion is also quite common. In the first term or year at school many children suddenly balk at the idea. A child who has been away from school through illness may often object to going back. What these children need is confidence, and parents can best give it to them by acting as if going to school were natural and normal and by showing little disturbance at the grizzling.

If the child is persistently unhappy about going to school, you probably ought to try to discover the reason. It may be a dislike of a particular teacher. It may be a question of persistent bullying in the playground. It may be something quite irrational. You can ask the child about it, although he may not be too keen to explain. If this is the case, try not to hold too many dreadful family conferences. Consult the teacher, of course, and try to pick up clues from the conversation of other children. There is usually something quite simple that can be done to put matters right.

There are also occasions when children simply play truant and go off for the afternoon. You may be worried by this, if only because it means that neither you nor the school knows where the child is. Mild truancy, like mild stealing, should be discouraged but not agonized over. If you and the school are aware of it you will both be a little more alert, and the child will find it correspondingly difficult to get off.

The most serious difficulty in this line is known as school phobia, which a child is said to be suffering from when he seriously and irrationally fears school. Such a child needs expert help. The cause of his fear often has nothing to do with school, and the child himself very rarely knows what it is he is afraid of. If time and the sympathy of teachers and parents do not seem to be working, you should seek the help of the school psychiatric service.

Of course, school phobia is only one of the many ways in which the effect of tension, anxiety or emotional disturbance becomes obvious. An enormous number of learning difficulties have emotional roots. Serious upset or unhappiness in the family, the loss of one parent, through death or divorce, unhappy home conditions like overcrowding can all, understandably enough, make stability and success at school difficult. One is alerted to the problem usually by the behaviour of the child. Some may riot and bully. Others may reject authority. Others may become lethargic and take refuge in stupidity. Obviously, if you have problems like these you will want to talk them over with the school, but equally obviously you may seek professional help. The school will be able to suggest the first steps you should take.

Many parents are puzzled by the difference between a psychiatrist and a psychologist. A child psychiatrist is a doctor who has had additional training in dealing with emotional and behavioural problems of children. A psychologist is not a doctor, but is trained to deal with the causes and treatment of learning problems and in testing intelligence and aptitude. Obviously the work of the psychiatrist and the psychologist may well overlap. A child with learning difficulties may be referred first to a psychologist and then, if the problem seems to be deep-seated, to a psychiatrist. A parent or teacher may want to consult a psychologist to get help in distinguishing between minor difficulties which are a normal part of development and more serious ones for which further help is needed. The psychologist is familiar with the whole range of normal behaviour and can thus give a better idea of how abnormal a particular child's behaviour may be. It is often comforting to parents to discover that a difficulty over which they had been agonizing was one which had been successfully faced by very large numbers of others.

Parents who consult a psychiatrist for their child may often find that he spends a comparatively short time with the child and rather a long time with one or both parents. This is a recognition of the fact that emotional and behavioural problems have their origins not only in the child himself but in his family background and circumstances.

There is an enormous range of behaviour problems for which you may seek help. Some children become difficult to control and are classified as maladjusted. For maladjusted children the school will no doubt suggest attendance at a child guidance clinic, where a psychiatrist will be in attendance. The child may be placed in a special class for maladjusted children or it may be suggested that he goes to a special school. More seriously disturbed children are described as 'psychotic'. Such children are so disturbed as to find it very difficult to relate to what is going on around them. A form of psychosis has become increasingly familiar under the name of autism. Autistic children tend not to communicate with others and may not develop the ability to speak. They present problems both for this reason and because they may be prey to storms of anger. These serious disorders are usually obvious before a child goes to school, but once of school age, the child can be served by the clinics and special schools provided by the education and medical services. Unhappily, the extent and quality of the service varies enormously from one part of the country to another and there is undoubtedly an enormous shortage of psychiatrists, psychologists and social workers. This is not to say that parents should be reluctant to use the services if necessary – but to warn them that they may have to be energetic and persistent in getting the attention required.

Learning Difficulties

There are some children to whom school seems to present no problems of any kind. Their books are covered with gratifying ticks and expressions of approval. They bring home sycophantic reports. Worse, they seem to achieve all this without paying much attention. Most children, however, are not like this. Most find difficulty at some point, and for some the difficulties may be serious. Many children are slow to read, and many more never really master mathematics. Any child may find a particular subject something of a torment. The first thing to do in difficulties of this kind is to have a word with the teacher, and we have discussed doing this in Chapters 6 and 10. The important thing here is to discover how serious the problem is and then to make sure that you and the school are working together to solve it. Many parents find that they are not the best people to help their own children: there is too much emotion involved. But if you are going to arrange extra help, through private lessons, do be sure that this too is working with rather than against what the school is doing. The argument for additional help is not just that it involves the child in extra effort and practice. It is that in learning anything there is usually a clue which makes the whole process easier. If the school hasn't offered this clue, it is possible that someone else might. We have all had the experience of seeing our way suddenly through a difficulty because someone has talked about it in a fresh way.

Another reason for being alert for difficulty is that many learning problems have physical causes. It may be hard to imagine, but it is a fact that a lot of children who were thought to be stupid or backward have turned out to be partially sighted or partially hearing. The physical defect may be not so obvious as to draw attention to itself, but it may be enough to inhibit understanding and learning. We shall be discussing physical disabilities in themselves later in this chapter, and we shall see that their swift diagnosis and treatment may prevent a good deal of difficulty at school.

Sometimes a child's difficulties may go beyond a slowness in reading or inability to master a specific subject. Backwardness may be associated with poor teaching, overcrowded classes, changes of school, frequent absences or something in the family background. It may also be related to a less than average intelligence, physical disorder or maladjustment. The first group of causes can be treated. For example, a school may group together a number of children who are slow to read and have them taught in small 'remedial' groups. This kind of special attention can often bring a child to the point where he can join in fruitfully in the work of normal classes. Similarly, if the child has been away from school a lot, or if you have had to move about frequently, you can help him to 'catch up' by judicious help at home arranged in consultation with the school. The difficulties whose roots lie more specifically within the child himself can also be tackled through the various child guidance services mentioned in this chapter.

There is one particular form of learning difficulty which has become more familiar lately under the name of 'dyslexia' or 'word blindness'. Some experts do not feel this can be readily distinguished from general reading difficulties and some wonder whether it is not just a comforting middle-class term for children who can't read. On the other hand, there are those who believe that dyslexic children do have a specific difficulty in relating visual symbols (letters and words) with spoken speech sounds and that these children also tend to be slow in learning to talk, have spatial defects, have difficulties in physical coordination and confuse left and right. There is some evidence that the condition is genetically determined, and that it is commoner in boys. For practical purposes the argument about a specific disability is not of great importance. What matters is that the child should get the proper treatment, and although provision is patchy, parents should not hesitate to seek help through the school and the medical services.

Perhaps one ought to add here that it is becoming increasingly common to regard the condition of autism as having a physical rather than a specifically emotional origin. Clearly it shares with dyslexia the disorder of language development.

It may be that a child has more than a specific difficulty – his overall development may be behind. A child who is noticeably backward may be classified as educationally subnormal, in which case he may go into a special class in the school, or it may be recommended that he go to a special school. Children who are even more seriously handicapped than this may be thought unsuitable for education in school at all. In the past they were even the responsibility of the health, rather than the education authorities. Since 1970, however, the education authority has had the responsibility for the education of such children whether they are at home or in hospital. Provision here varies enormously, and it ought to be stated bluntly that the conditions under which some mentally handicapped children live are appallingly bad.

The towering problems which face the parents of mentally handicapped children are beyond the scope of this book, but if you are in this position you should seek the help of perhaps the very best voluntary organization of parents in the country: the National Society for Mentally Handicapped Children.

Physical Difficulties

There remains the whole range of physical disabilities. There are ten categories of handicap which are recognized officially and for which special schools are available. One of them is educational subnormality and another maladjustment – which have been mentioned earlier. The others are blindness, partial sight, deafness, partial hearing, physical handicap, delicacy, epilepsy and speech defects. In the physically handicapped and delicate categories come such disabilities as cerebral palsy, spina bifida, muscular dystrophy, the after-effects of polio, heart disease and limb deformities. Hidden among the overall statistics are the depressing numbers of children injured in road accidents.

Parents whose children are handicapped in some way probably need no urging to get the best and earliest possible diagnosis and then to seek whatever treatment is appropriate and available. Very often a child who is physically handicapped has, understandably enough, some emotional difficulties as well, so it may not be enough just to treat the disability itself.

There has been a continuing debate over the years as to whether it is better for children with handicaps of all kinds (mental, physical or emotional) to be educated separately or alongside their contemporaries. The argument for separate special schools is that the handicap can be treated by experienced people, usually in smaller groups and with more generous pupil–teacher ratios. The argument against is that the children are cut off from normal life and find the transition difficult and painful when they leave school. It is probable that, as conditions in schools generally improve, as remedial and special classes become more common, there will be an increasing tendency to keep handicapped children in the normal education service.

Where you can turn for help

There are two main sources of help for parents with children who have problems: the first is the school itself and the education service behind it; the second is the host of voluntary agencies, many of them set up by parents themselves.

Through the school you can have access to educational psychologists, child psychiatrists and child guidance clinics, to the school welfare service and to the school medical and dental officers. You can be put in touch with special schools and provision for the handicapped. If for some reason you do not wish to approach these agencies through the school, get in touch direct with the local education office whose address you can find from your local library.

There are other agencies, run not by the education authorities but by the social service departments of local authorities. These have recently been reorganized and it should be possible to get help across the wide range of local authority services from the local office of the social service department. Parents with serious worries or problems concerning the family, their marriage, housing or money should find someone at the local office competent to make a start in dealing with them.

Even when you have been in touch with the publicly provided services you may find it helpful to contact or join a voluntary organization. The advantage of this is that it gives you the support that can come from meeting people with similar problems to your own and with access to additional help. The list below is not exhaustive but it does cover the main areas of problems and handicaps covered in the chapter.

British Epilepsy Association, 3 Alfred Place, London WC1, 01-580 2704.

Catholic Handicapped Children's Fellowship, 2 The Villas, Hare Law, Stanley, Co. Durham, Annfield Plain 379.

Chest and Heart Association, Tavistock House North, Tavistock Square, London WC1, 01-387 3012.

Family Service Units, 207 Old Marylebone Road, London NW1, 01-723 0218.

Invalid Children's Aid Association, 126 Buckingham Palace Road, London SW1, 01-730 9891.

Muscular Dystrophy Group, 26 Borough High Street, London SE1, 01-407 5116.

National Association for Gifted Children, 27 John Adam Street, London WC2, 01-930 7731.

National Association for Mental Health, 39 Queen Anne Street, London W1, 01-935 1272.

National Deaf Children's Society, 31 Gloucester Place, London W1, 01-486 3251.

National Society for Autistic Children, 1a Golders Green Road, London NW11, 01-458 4375.

National Society for Mentally Handicapped Children, 86 Newman Street, London W1, 01-636 2861.

Royal National Institute for the Blind, 224 Great Portland Street, London W1, 01-387 5571.

Spastics Society, 12 Park Crescent, London W1, 01-636 5020.

Spina Bifida Trust, 112 City Road, London EC1, 01-253 2735.

12 Whom to Chivvy

Education is a personal matter. It succeeds or fails with children, not with systems. But if something is not right, the system is what you have to change or influence. Unfortunately, the system can seem large and complex: authority assumes many varied aspects. If a parent wants something, who is competent to advise or decide? Is it the teacher, the head, the education officer, the 'committee', the Department of Education and Science – or someone else? It sometimes seems to parents as if all these official people are in a conspiracy to deny his wishes and to make him and his child conform to arrangements designed for somebody else's convenience. A parent who is overwhelmed by the special problems of his own child has to make his way through a jungle of laws, regulations and officials to discover who is responsible for what and who has the power of decision. Some unhappy parents waste a great deal of time and energy nagging away at the wrong place, trying to get a concession or a decision out of people who are not competent to give it.

It is not only individuals who need to know their way about the education service. Increasingly parents are taking a greater interest in education through such pressure groups as parents' associations and associations 'for the advancement of state education'. Many of these groups have discovered that they are more successful in arguing for what they want if they have a clear idea of what is possible to the people they are arguing with. It is, for example, bad tactics to spend a lot of time blackguarding the local authorities, especially in public, for something which is the responsibility of the Secretary of State.

There are five main sources of decision in education: the law, the courts, the Secretary of State for Education and Science, the local education authorities and the schools themselves. What is done in education is the responsibility of one of these five. Let us look at them in turn, beginning with the schools, which are nearest to the personal experience of most parents.

The Schools

Most of what happens to children in the English education service is the responsibility of the particular school to which they go. In this we differ from many other countries where a curriculum or methods of discipline may be laid down centrally and even by law. In Britain, what a child is taught and the methods by which he is taught it are a matter for his teachers. The new methods described in earlier chapters, new kinds of examinations and new subjects in the curriculum are all introduced (or not introduced) by a decision of teachers, not of the local or national authorities. So there is a whole range of issues on which a parent who is worried or irritated should take the matter up directly with the school – and the ease and pleasure of doing so will be affected by the school's attitude to parents and the arrangements it makes for meeting them. (See Chapter 10.)

It may be useful to mention some of the points that can arise. You may discover that your child's infant school is organized on 'family grouping' lines – that is, that children of the whole age range from five to eight work together in the same class. You may not be convinced by the arrangement and feel that it is unsuitable for your own child. You may wish to revert to the more familiar arrangement where children 'go up' every year as they get older. Or you may feel that you are a 'progressive' parent who has read all the arguments against streaming children by ability and that you wish to see it abolished in your child's school. You may wish that a school made more effective use of the cane, because children these days need discipline – or you may object to the fact that the cane is used at all (albeit under regulations devised by the local authority). With a secondary school child you may wish that additional science or a particular modern language was available. You may object to the choices that your child is required to make between various subjects. You may want him to be entered for an external examination, when the school has decided that he could not manage the course. You may feel that a school's demands about uniform are unreasonable or that a headmaster is carrying his feelings about length of hair or skirts to the point of fetish.

In all these instances you have to persuade the school to do what you want. The most usual method is to go along and talk to the head or the teachers. If you find that a number of other parents have the same worry as yourself you may want to get together to make your point – but teachers are wary of this sort of pressure and many react badly to it. You may find you get further as individuals. If the school will not do as you ask there is usually very little you can do about it. You can appeal to the governors, but they are most unlikely to pressure the staff. You can talk to the local education authority, but both officials and elected members are likely to tell you that these things are a matter for the schools themselves. Indeed, the main point of going to the local education office would be to discover if there is a place in another school, more to your liking to which your child could be transferred. On the whole, if a decision is within the competence of the school itself, what you have to rely on is tact, charm and persuasion, though there is no need to begin by assuming that these will not in many cases be successful. Teachers may be prickly about pressure but they are often reasonably amenable to suggestion and ready to do what they can to help. If you fail, and continue to feel strongly, the only thing you can do is to move the child to another school. But usually the best advice in these circumstances is 'relax'. In the end, it is almost certainly more important that your child should be happy and confident at and about school than that any particular point of principle should be established.

There is one other point in the individual school where you can at least begin chivvying if things are not as they should be. Every school has a board of managers (for primary schools) or governors (for secondary schools) – though in some authorities several schools are grouped under single boards. The governors have three kinds of duties: decision, oversight and pressure. Their powers of decision are exercised in appointing staff and in disciplinary cases like the suspension of pupils. Their overseeing duties include responsibility for the conduct and curriculum of the school (though the day to day responsibility is the head's) and the approval of estimates. As for pressure, they have a duty to keep an eye on the state of the buildings and tell the local authority if something needs to be done. But they can also help in any battle with the authority on the allocation of resources. Some authorities are now appointing both teachers and parents (and a few pupils) to be governors of their own schools.

An example of a small but important difference which governors can make is the conversion of some wasted nook into a store cupboard. This seemingly trivial act can often make a world of difference to the sports or music provision of a school, and give the children and a teacher heart to develop a specific interest. Good ideas can falter in a school if they have to be carried out in inconvenience and confusion. Often the headmaster can get changes like this made by having a word with the education office, but the backing of the governors can also be a help.

Governors and managers are seen as a pressure group most typically when a school needs some fairly major improvement or extension. Parents and teachers may be enraged by the condition of the outside lavatories. To improve or abolish them may mean getting a place in the minor works building programme. The interest of the governors here can be quite crucial, both in their corporate capacity and as members of various committees and sub-committees. If you wish to agitate for improvement, it is a good thing to have the governors or managers on your side, and you will normally find them very ready to help.

Local Education Authorities

It is clear from what I have been saying about individual schools and their boards of governors or managers that very great responsibilities in education rest with the local education authorities. These are the councils of the new counties, the metropolitan districts, the outer London boroughs and the anomalous Inner London Education Authority. (Until 1974, county boroughs were education authorities too.) It is through them that the education service is largely operated. In fact, British education has been described as a national service, locally administered. So there are a whole lot of parental worries which can be settled, not at the school, but at the local education office.

Under the 1944 Act the local education authorities have the duty 'so far as their powers extend, to contribute to the spiritual, moral, mental and physical development of the community by securing that sufficient education . . . shall be available . . .'. Specifically, they have a large number of duties, from providing enough adequate schools to cleansing verminous pupils and appointing a chief education officer. They also have a large number of powers, from controlling secular education to inspecting schools or compulsorily purchasing land for school building. Their powers and duties are in fact laid down in the Education Act, 1944 and in subsequent Education Acts. The people ultimately responsible for all this are the elected councillors of the local authority. But they are required by law to appoint an education committee which may consist both of themselves and of coopted members. The education committee may in turn appoint a number of sub-committees – for example, for primary, secondary and further education. The work of these elected and coopted members is of course voluntary.

The permanent paid officials of a local education authority are headed by a chief education officer or director of education. Under him are deputies and assistants, inspectors, advisers and the whole hierarchy of officials and clerks.

Many parents are not quite sure whom they should get in touch with if they wish to raise a matter which is the responsibility of the local education authority. Of course, ideally they should be able to go to the local education office and get this information, but offices vary in the degree of competence and helpfulness which they display to enquirers. Very broadly, you should tackle the officials if your problem lies within the policy and practice laid down by the authority. You should tackle the elected or coopted members if you want the policy or practice changed.

The most usual occasion for a parent's visit to the local education office is a move from one school to another. This most often creates difficulty at the point of transfer from primary to secondary schools and the conflict between parental choice and the eleven plus. This has been more fully covered in Chapter 7. So we can take as an example here the case of a parent who moves into a local authority's area and wishes to discuss the schools to which his child may go. There will usually be no policy to contend with: it will be a matter of discovering where there is a vacant place. As good schools tend to be popular, the vacant places may be most readily available in schools which parents may want to avoid. What parents usually do is move into their new house, look for the local primary school and turn up there with the child; and usually this works. But sometimes parents don't like the look of the local primary school and so look further afield. Some parents may even go to the education office to ask for a list of schools so that they can do this in a systematic way. The point is that at some stage you may find yourself talking to officials either to find out about local schools or to persuade them to let your child go to the school of your choice. In these circumstances it is best to assume that you will be received with courtesy and friendliness. And it certainly helps if you know who it is you want to see. Many parents make the mistake of simply turning up at the town hall and putting their problem to the nearest official. Very often they get hold of somebody who is not in a position to help, either because he or she is too junior or because he is from a quite different department. If you wish to go to the education office, find out from the local library who is responsible for the field in which you are interested and make an appointment to see him. If it is a question of choosing a school or wanting to transfer to another one you could start with the assistant education officer or deputy education officer responsible for schools. He may pass you on to his deputy, but at least you will have started in the right place. If you do suspect that the official with whom you are dealing is not able to give you an answer, or that he is stalling in some way, then do not hesitate to ask firmly and courteously to see the person responsible. Be ready to make an appointment if necessary.

You may of course feel that the officials are being unhelpful, or that their suggestions are unsatisfactory. Your remedy here lies through the elected members of the authority. The obvious person to get onto is your local councillor on the education authority. He himself may be a member of the education committee, or of the relevant sub-committee, but in any case he can put you in touch with somebody who is. You can find out who your councillors and committee members are at the local library.

The point about going to a councillor is not to have a battle with the officials nor to try to bring some additional pressure to bear. Usually the official will be trying to work within what he understands to be the rules – though it is true that some can be simply obstinate and unhelpful. The point about going to the elected members is that it is they who are ultimately responsible under our system of administration.

It is the council which carries the can, decides how rules can be interpreted and whether exceptions can be made. So it is entirely right, if you get into an impasse with the officials, that you should seek a way out through the elected representatives. The officers act only within the decisions taken by the council or its committees, so if you want some special treatment or consideration, which the officer cannot allow, or you believe that you have been hardly dealt with, the people to get in touch with are the elected members.

It may be, of course, that in seeking some limited and personal decision for your own child, you actually come up against a decision that the committee has taken. You may find that it is impossible to do what you want within the existing rules. And you may feel strongly enough about it to want the rules changed. Here there really is not much sense in attacking the officials. You can of course try to persuade them that the point you are making is a genuine one and that they ought to suggest to the committee that a change in the rules should be made. But if you are determined, you will at some stage have to tackle the committee itself. If the point you are making really is a genuine one, then you will no doubt find a number of other parents ready to campaign with you. An example may help here. Supposing you believe very strongly in the virtues of educating boys and girls separately, in different schools (a belief shared by the traditional English middle classes and immigrant communities from India and Pakistan). You may suddenly find that the local authority proposes, as part of a scheme of reorganization, to enlarge a local boys' school and girls' school and turn them into two mixed schools. You may object that this makes it impossible for your children to get the education you believe in, and you may find a lot of local parents share your views. There are, of course, a number of different suggestions and arguments you might be able to put. It might be, for example, that your authority will continue to have a number of single-sex schools in other parts of its area – so your campaign might be directed simply to establishing your right to choose these schools for your children. On the other hand, there may be no such schools, or they may be too far away, so you and your fellow-parents might wish to try to stop the proposed change altogether. The thing to remember is that this kind of decision is within the discretion of a local education authority, so you have to persuade the authority to change its mind.

You will naturally, first of all, seek to understand exactly what is proposed. A local authority which wishes in effect to change the character of a school has to give notice of its intention to do so and give time for objections. It is open to you at this point to have discussions with officials to make sure you understand the plans. The official will defend the decision of the committee and tell you the reasons for it. What is more, he may himself be committed to it, having worked on the plan for some months; indeed, he may have suggested it himself to the committee as a solution to some of its problems. You can seek to change his mind, and he may agree to put your points before the committee. But he is not ultimately responsible, so if you are going to throw a tantrum you should save it for a more appropriate moment.

Tackling the education committee calls into play all the normal lobbying tactics of the democratic process. You write to councillors and committee members, invite them to meetings, public or private, you write letters to the press, you get up petitions. If you suspect that the governors of the schools concerned are unhappy about the proposal, you seek to stiffen their resistance. You may, of course, seek to persuade the committee of the rightness of your cause by the simple reasonableness of your argument, but ultimately the weapon which you have is votes. Local councillors come up for re-election – and in local elections only about a third of the electorate votes, so if you can raise a big enough noise you can make councillors wonder how far opposition to what you want is worth it. Even people who do not agree with you may get the impression from your campaign that the local authority has made a bit of a mess of things.

On the other hand, you should recall, in the quiet intervals while you are licking envelopes between meetings, that you are probably interested in a relatively narrow point – in this example, your desire for single-sex schools. The local authority will quite certainly have considered this when drawing up its proposals, but it will have had to consider a whole lot of other things as well, like the availability of buildings, the pressure of government policy, the need to provide a full range of courses for all. To the committee and the officials it may well seem that a vociferous campaign on a narrow point should not be allowed to succeed because it endangers the achievement of other goals which are at least equally important. One can never have perfection, and it may have been a very reasonable judgement that coeducation was a small price to pay for a lot of other advantages. They may even be able to argue, with justice, that your success would make it harder for them to offer a decent education to the other children for whom they are responsible. You may regard yourself and your campaign in terms of St George setting out to see off the dragon. From other points of view, it may be that you and your colleagues are the baddies.

This is a commonplace of democratic action, and one which might well sort itself out as the campaign proceeds. The point is that our local system of educational administration offers an opportunity for people in a locality to make their views known and to object if they want to. It enables administrators to know how far their plans are acceptable and to gain consent for them. The opportunities are there to be used but perhaps it is appropriate, in a book addressed primarily to parents, to suggest that parents can often be wrong, especially about their own children. And remember that if you fight an acrimonious battle and lose, it may be that your children will be going in the end to a school which they know you fought hard to keep them out of.

Of course, the subject on which you feel strongly and wish to campaign may not involve attacking an authority's plans for organizing schools. You may believe that your child's school is getting an unfair share of resources. To take a specific example, you may feel that the arrangements for school games or for swimming are inadequate. You may find that the headmaster shares your general principle that swimming is important and games desirable. The provision of playing fields and visits to the local baths (especially if these require transport) are the responsibility of the local authority. You and your fellow parents may well wish to mount a campaign about this – and you may find that your hand is strengthened if parents from other schools join in. It is often better if you can be seen to be pressing for general improvement as well as specific treatment. The principle, however, is the same, whatever the size of the issue. If you want to get a decision out of the education committee, or change a decision they have made, concentrate on the elected members.

The Law and the Government

The local education authorities have, as we have seen, very wide responsibilities for education, and a great deal of discretion, but these responsibilities are conferred upon them by law, and they can act only within the powers and duties which the law gives them. What is more, they are subject to the overall direction of the Secretary of State for Education and Science, who is a member of the government. This means that there are a number of instances where a parent may find himself faced with a legal requirement or a ruling of the courts or a regulation of the Secretary of State, and it is to these national institutions that we must now turn.

What happens in education, as in other spheres of national life, is ultimately the responsibility of Parliament. Parliament makes laws laying down the national policy for education and determining how it should be controlled and administered.

Parliament votes more than half the money spent on education (in common with other local government services) and gives the government power to control expenditure financed from elsewhere. It is from Parliament too that the authority of ministers derives, and Members of Parliament keep a general watch on education through debates and parliamentary questions.

All decisions are based ultimately on the law which Parliament makes – that is upon the Education Act of 1944 and about a dozen smaller Acts since. When individuals make decisions, whether they are teachers, an official at County Hall, a civil servant or the Secretary of State, they do so on the basis of the law. None of them can agree to something prohibited by law or refuse a right which is granted by it. For example, full-time education from five to sixteen (the latter since 1972), at school or elsewhere, is compulsory. No authority, from the lowest to the highest, can compel a child to have full-time education before or after the legal age. Nor can any of them agree to a child's remaining out of full-time education while he is of the compulsory age. A mother may feel very strongly that her five-year-old cannot manage a full day at school, but she cannot legally keep him out of school for part of the day, nor can a school legally agree to such an arrangement. On those occasions where the procedure is allowed the law is quite simply broken. Similarly, a parent cannot remove a child from school early to take a job, whatever the need of the parent, the attraction of the job or the unhappiness of the child at school. In a matter like this the Secretary of State has no more discretion than the school or the welfare officer. They are all bound by the Act of Parliament. So is the parent, and if he objects he can only break the law by taking the child away from school and hoping the local authority will not prosecute – or in the long term by changing the law itself.

A good example of the way in which the Secretary of State is bound by law is given by the question of raising the school-leaving age. The Secretary of State could raise the age to sixteen in 1972, without legislation, because the 1944 Act provides for it. But when the government wanted to establish two leaving dates a year instead of three, while the age remained at fifteen, it could not do so until it passed the Education Act, 1962.

The upshot of all this is that if you want some action to be taken or stopped, some right acknowledged, or an abuse remedied, your first step is to see what the Education Acts say on the subject. If the question is unambiguously covered by an Act of Parliament, there is not very much you or anybody else can do about it, at least in the short term.

But not all Acts of Parliament are unambiguous. Some of them are badly framed. Others are out of date. Or the various sections of an Act may have become inconsistent as a result of amendments on its passage through Parliament. Or one Act may be inconsistent with another. An Act may need interpretation as to what Parliament really meant or as to its relation with the legal principles of society. It may be simply inadequate: circumstances may arise which were not foreseen when the original legislation was passed. In all these circumstances authoritative decisions are given by the courts. It is not just that the courts passively interpret legislation: in effect they make law. This is one of the ways in which the law is kept flexible and usable. This means that people giving decisions on behalf of authority have to do so within the framework of the rulings of the courts as well as of Acts of Parliament.

Again, some examples may help. The Education Acts have laid down the 'statutory walking distance' for children: up to the age of eight it is two miles, and over eight it is three miles. Under the statutory walking distance a local authority cannot be compelled to pay bus fares or provide transport: above that distance it must. But how do you measure three miles? Is it along a road, across a field, the way the bus goes, from the doorstep or from a bus stop? Can the authority pay half the fare, or merely the part over two or three miles?

What if there are no pavements or if traffic is especially dangerous? And what if one child lives just under the three miles from a school, his friend lives just over three miles and the bus stop is in the middle? Obviously shoals of particular problems arise from a seemingly simple enactment, and on all of them the courts have ruled. They have decided, for example, that a route need not be a road, and that distance, not safety, is the test for deciding the nearest available route.

Or let us take the compulsory school age again. The law says that a child becomes of statutory age at the beginning of the term when he reaches the age of five. But when does a child reach that age, and what about the child who is five on the first day of term? The courts have ruled on this too: a person attains a given age at the beginning of the day which is the anniversary of his birth. So the child who was five on the first day of term was legally five just before the term started.

There is one particular legal decision which is of great importance to those parents who want to choose the school to which their child should go. The case of Watt v. Kesteven County Council, 1955 showed how weak were parents' rights under Section 76 of the 1944 Act (see Chapter 3) by pointing out that the section does not say that pupils must in all cases be educated in accordance with the wishes of their parents. The court said that the section laid down a general principle to which the local education authority must have regard – leaving it open to the authority to have regard to other things as well and also to make exceptions to the general principle if it thinks fit.

Another, more recent, decision of the courts was even more puzzling. In the summer of 1967 a group of people in Enfield tried to stop the local scheme of secondary reorganization by claiming that the local authority had ignored the procedure laid down in Section 13 of the 1944 Act. The judgement turned on whether the local authority, in converting a grammar school and a secondary modern school into a senior and junior comprehensive school respectively, was in effect ceasing to maintain two schools and establishing two others. The judge said the authority would be doing so if it were making a change in the fundamental character of the schools. But what constitutes such a change? The judge held that simply changing a grammar or secondary modern school into a comprehensive school was not in itself changing the fundamental character – but changing the age range (admitting pupils at fourteen instead of eleven) or taking in pupils of a different sex was. The judgement was remote from educational experience and common sense, but there it is, and the Education Act 1968 was passed to make all these changes legally changes of character.

It is clear then that a parent seeking enlightenment about his own particular situation should consult not only the Education Acts, but the decisions of the courts. And lest this sounds a very formidable undertaking, I should say at once that there is a very handy guide, *The New Law of Education*, by Taylor and Saunders, described later in this chapter, which ought to be available in every public library.

It is of course the law – the Education Act, 1944 – that has created both a Secretary of State and a Department of Education and Science. The duty of the Secretary of State is 'to promote the education of the people of England and Wales and the progressive development of institutions devoted to that purpose, and to secure the effective execution by local authorities, under his control and direction, of the national policy for providing a varied and comprehensive educational service in every area'. By an Order in Council of March 1964 the Secretary of State and the Department were given all the responsibilities of the former Minister and Ministry of Education together with responsibility for the universities and civil science. Although the wording of the Act makes the Secretary of State sound pretty powerful, there are a number of reasons why this impression is slightly misleading. In the first place these general statements in Acts of Parliament are legally vacuous. Indeed, the existence of legislation in effect limits the power of ministers. It works like this. All of us are held by the law to be 'natural persons': we can do anything that is not specifically prohibited by law. (This deep-seated principle distinguishes English law from that of many other countries, where people are given specific rights. In England, it is assumed that everybody has rights – to do anything which is legal.) Any minister acts as an agent of the Queen, and because he is a 'corporation sole', the civil servants acting in his name are in effect the Queen's agents too. Now the Queen is a natural person in legal terms, and so she – and her ministers – can do anything that is not prohibited by law. In this sense ministers can do what they like. But English law has come to act as a check upon the centralizing power of ministers, and there is another important legal principle to the effect that if the government takes a statutory power to do something in a limited field, it cannot claim to behave like a natural person in the rest of the field. In other words, if a minister takes a specific narrow power by law, he cannot take wider powers in the same field without further legislation. The reasoning behind this is genuinely legalistic. It is that if the power of a natural person actually existed in the wider field then there was no need for legislation in the narrower. The very existence of legislation in the narrower field implies the need for legislation in the wider. The problem for departments of state in framing legislation is to give their ministers the power to do what the ministers require without either tying their hands too much for the future or coming up with the sort of legislation passed by Henry VIII (which tended to give him the power to do what he liked whenever he liked to anybody he disliked). What this means, in brief, is that ministers are bound by their own legislation, just like the rest of us. They can do, normally, only what the law gives them power to do.

A second reason why the Secretary of State is less omnipotent than the Act might seem to imply is that legislation so far has given expression to the principle that the education service rests upon a partnership between the Secretary of State, the local authorities and such voluntary bodies as religious denominations. This is why most of what goes on in education is the responsibility of local education authorities. It is what makes it possible for you as a parent to chivvy some responsible person in your own locality.

But, of course, there is a great deal that a Secretary of State does do, and many ways in which parents wanting something have to take account of his decisions. These include his role in making national policy, his power to issue regulations and circulars and his partly judicial position as an arbiter between parents and local authorities.

The Secretary of State's role in policy making is normally expressed in Acts of Parliament, regulations and the like which are discussed later in this chapter. But there are places where a parent may bump up against policy in general terms. For example, since the war there has been one Minister of Education who believed in the value of small village schools. Any parent or group of parents battling to save the local school, and carrying the campaign up to the Minister, would have found a more sympathetic ear at that time than at any other. Similarly, a particular Secretary of State might decide that most of the school-building programme ought to go to primary schools. A group of parents agitating to get a primary school replaced will find the context of national policy more helpful here than a similar group with a slum secondary school on their hands. The influence of policy can also be indirect. For example, if the government wants to reorganize secondary education, and a local authority's plan for this involves turning a boys' school into a mixed school, parents who object may find that for the Secretary of State the balance of advantage lies clearly with the authority. The lesson from all this is that, if you are going to invoke a Secretary of State in some way, find out what the policy is and frame your arguments in terms of it. Ministers tend to speak a lot, so there is normally some expression of policy or opinion that you can seize upon and quote to your advantage. You may have to comb through the newspapers fairly thoroughly for some time to find what you want, but if there has been a major statement of policy the press office at the Department of Education and Science will refer you to the date and the occasion.

Perhaps the major way in which Secretaries of State make known their policies and requirements is in what are called statutory rules, regulations and instruments. The Secretary of State can make regulations only when he has been given specific power to do so by Act of Parliament – but once they are made, regulations have the force of law. They are second in importance only to an Act itself. It is the Schools Regulations, 1959, which govern the repair of school premises, the size of classes, admission to schools, the length of the school year, school terms and holidays and the school day, and the appointment and qualifications of teachers. It was these Regulations which used to say, until recently amended, that the number of pupils on the register of a class should not exceed forty in primary schools and thirty in secondary schools – 'provided that if, owing to the shortage of teachers or other unavoidable circumstances, it is not possible to comply with the Regulation, the number of pupils on the register of any class shall be such as is reasonable in all the circumstances'.

The Regulations also give precision and detail to the brief and general requirements of the Act. For example, the Education Act, 1944, says that children of school age must have full-time education. Full-time is nowhere defined in the Act. The Schools Regulations lay down that for pupils under eight there must be at least three hours of secular instruction and for pupils over eight at least four hours, divided into two sessions, one in the morning and the other in the afternoon. They also say that schools shall meet for at least 400 sessions in each school year (that is, 200 days) though up to twenty days of 'occasional school holidays' may be deducted from this.

Another way in which a Secretary of State makes known his policies is by circulars, memoranda and so on. Many circulars simply explain regulations or relate to duties imposed by the Education Acts. Circulars and memoranda are not legally binding in themselves, but normally what a circular says goes. The point is that a local authority can argue with a circular: all it can do with a regulation is to induce the Secretary of State to bring out a new one.

Perhaps the most famous recent circular is Circular 10/65. It asserted the then government's policy for reorganizing secondary education on comprehensive lines and requested local authorities to prepare and submit plans for doing so. It then listed the kinds of schemes that would be acceptable. The point about this was that the government decided quite specifically not to legislate, and used a circular precisely because it would not have the force of law. The objective was to achieve reorganization by consent – and in this it was very largely successful. Another circular with which parents found themselves arguing was Circular 8/60, which said that no new state nursery schools should be established for the present. This Circular has itself been replaced with Circular 2/73, which provided for the expansion of nursery education.

The most numerous documents which the Secretary of State publishes are administrative memoranda. These are normally about matters of routine, but some are much more than this. For example, the 'Notes for Guidance' to local authorities on the establishment of polytechnics and the creation of independent governing bodies for them was an administrative memorandum – number 8/67.

One of the most interesting documents to parents comes under the category of circulars and memoranda but is in fact neither. It is the *Manual of Guidance, Schools* No. 1. In this the Secretary of State set out the principles governing a parent's choice of one school rather than another. It was not meant to be a substitute for the Secretary of State's consideration of individual cases, but it did give a good idea of the general principles he had in mind when deciding. The manual is now officially withdrawn (but see Chapter 3).

The *Manual of Guidance* brings us nicely to the Secretary of State's semi-judicial functions. There are all kinds of ways, under the Act, in which he is required to act as an arbiter. For example, in a dispute between a local authority and a parent, the Secretary of State may decide to which school a particular child may go. He may also determine any dispute between a local education authority and the managers or governors of a school. It is also possible to complain to the Secretary or State that a local authority is acting unreasonably – thought it is in practice very difficult to show this. If you are thinking of tackling the local authority by appealing to the Secretary of State, perhaps through your local M.P., it would be as well to look up what has happened in the past to see whether or not you are likely to be wasting your time. The guiding principle is that if a local authority is doing something which it has the power or duty to do, a Secretary of State is most unlikely to override its judgement.

Conclusions

These, then, are the authorities in education, the people you should harry if things go wrong. You can see that authority comes in many forms. What you want done, or not done, may be the responsibility of the school, the local authority or the Secretary of State. All these operate within a framework of the law. There is no need, however, to be put off. In practice most things can be settled either directly with a teacher or the head of a school – or at worst with the local education office. But don't be too daunted if it seems that you have to take on the remoter authorities as well. The thing to do is know where you're going. Don't waste time in unproductive argument. Find out who is responsible and tackle them directly. To do this you need to spend an hour or two in the public library. The strategy is first of all to see what the law is, and second what the courts have ruled. You then need to see if the matter is covered in regulations, circulars and so on. You should check whether something is within the discretion of the local authority. You might think that this is almost a full-time research job, but fortunately help is at hand. There is a single book, called *The New Law of Education* by G. Taylor and J. B. Saunders. Supplements are issued periodically to keep it up to date. This book is a marvel of its kind. It not only quotes all the major Acts in full, but by means of notes to each section refers you to the decisions of the courts and to regulations and so on. The book also includes the most important regulations, circulars and memoranda. And at the beginning, there is an introduction which covers the whole ground in a basic and helpful fashion. Without such a book it would have been almost frivolous to suggest to parents that they should themselves try to understand the law and the authorities in education. With Taylor and Saunders, parents too can be experts.

One final point. If you start a campaign or an appeal, it is entirely possible to become obsessed by the process. Personal and voluntary action of this kind takes an enormous amount of energy, enthusiasm and concentration. You may get carried away by the momentum of your own campaign. So it might be worth concluding this chapter by reminding ourselves gently that the campaign is not an end in itself. The central priority is the children and their experience at school. It would be a pity if they got lost in the wash. It may be that a graceful compromise is in their best interests, even though it means fudging a point of principle. Remember that most things in education are a matter of controversy and debate. It has not been certainly established what is best for children, let alone what is best for individual children. So before spending the best years of your life battling with the Secretary of State perhaps you should remember, if less dramatically, Cromwell's advice: 'I beseech you in the bowels of Christ, think it possible you may be mistaken.'

Index

More about Penguins and Pelicans

Penguinews, which appears every month, contains details of all the new books issued by Penguins as they are published. From time to time it is supplemented by *Penguins in Print*, which is our complete list of almost 5,000 titles.

A specimen copy of *Penguinews* will be sent to you free on request. Please write to Dept EP, Penguin Books Ltd, Harmondsworth, Middlesex, for your copy.

In the U.S.A.: For a complete list of books available from Penguin in the United States write to Dept CS, Penguin Books Inc., 7110 Ambassador Road, Baltimore, Maryland 21207.

In Canada: For a complete list of books available from Penguin in Canada write to Penguin Books Canada Ltd, 41 Steelcase Road West, Markham, Ontario.